KAMEN NEVENKIN

FROM LENINGRAD TO NARVA

AN ILLUSTRATED STUDY OF THE BATTLES IN THE NORTHERN BALTIC AREA

JANUARY - SEPTEMBER 1944

PUBLISHED BY
PeKo Publishing Kft.
8360 Keszthely, Bessenyei György utca 37.
Email: info@pekobooks.com
www.pekobooks.com

RESPONSIBLE PUBLISHER
Péter Kocsis

AUTHOR
Kamen Nevenkin

PRINTED IN HUNGARY

PHOTOS
NAC, RinP, TsAMO, National Archives of Norway, Mirko Bayerl, Georgy Lukin, Leonid Gorchakov, Kamen Nevenkin

FIRST PUBLISHED
2019

ISBN 978-615-5583-18-6

TABLE OF CONTENTS

CHAPTER 1

THE SIEGE OF LENINGRAD

THE GERMAN DRIVE TO THE GATES OF LENINGRAD

On 22 June 1941 Hitler's Third Reich invaded the Soviet Union. Three powerful Nazi army groups quickly annihilated the Red forces deployed along the border and raced across Russia's heartland. By mid-October most of Stalin's prewar regular army already had been destroyed and the Wehrmacht had advanced as far as Leningrad, Moscow, Kharkov and Crimea.

The northernmost of these army groups, Army Group 'North' (Heeresgruppe Nord), was led by Feldmarschall Wilhelm Ritter von Leeb. It consisted of two armies (16. and 18.) and a panzer group (4.), comprising 30 divisions, six of them armored or motorized. The army group was to receive close air support from the units of Air Fleet 1 (Luftflotte 1) totaling about 400 combat aircraft.

The mission of Army Group 'North' was to thrust from East Prussia, destroy the Red Army forces in the Baltic region, eliminate the bases of the Baltic Fleet, destroy what was left of Soviet naval power, capture Leningrad and eventually link up with the allied Finnish forces closing in from the northwest.

* * *

The offensive of Leeb's army group began with the first rays of light on 22 June. The two-pronged German offensive (18. Army on the left and 16. Army with 4. Panzer Group on the right) quickly smashed its way through the Soviet border defenses (Northwestern Front) and broke out into open country. Over the next two weeks all of Lithuania and Latvia together with southern Estonia fell into their hands. The defeated Soviets fell back in disarray, leaving behind a multitude of equipment and heavy weapons.

By 10 July the spearheads of Army Group 'North' reached Pärnu, Tartu and Pskov. It seemed that that ultimate victory was on the horizon – at the rate the German forward detachments were advancing they would need about a week to enter Leningrad. But all of a sudden fresh Soviet reserves appeared on the battlefield (including marines and sailors from the Baltic Fleet) stiffening Soviet resistance and the German offensive began to lose momentum. The Soviet counterattacks at Staraya Russa proved to be especially dangerous. Even though they were parried by the 16. Army and the panzer group, the latter failed to gain much more ground and, by 17-18 July, was halted by the Kingisepp - Luga defensive position. Thus, von Leeb fell short of taking the city on the run in July when the weather was still warm and the terrain allowed quick movements of large mechanized formations.

The Red forces occupying the Kingisepp - Luga position were now the only barrier between Army Group 'North' and Leningrad. Strict orders were given by the Soviet leadership for the city to be held at any cost. The former imperial capital of Russia, however, was literally defenseless because Stalin's high command never expected a threat to Leningrad from the west/southwest and had no field fortifications in that direction. It was the fierce resistance put up by the defenders of Kingisepp and Luga that bought precious time for about 500,000 men and women busy digging trenches and constructing bunkers around the city. Their efforts fully paid off and when, in the first days of September 1941, von Leeb's divisions finally penetrated into the suburbs they ran into an impregnable web of trench lines, anti-tank ditches and weapon emplacements.

* * *

On 21 July the German High Command finally realized that the Kingisepp – Luga position could not be penetrated on the run. That's why Hitler and his aides decided to change their strategy – instead of delivering a powerful strike on Leningrad with little regard to the flanks, it was decided to consolidate the forces on both wings, clear the rest of Estonia and the Novgorod area, and only then to renew the offensive on the old Russian Imperial Capital. In order to increase the striking power of the army group, the powerful VIII. Air Corps (VIII. Fliegerkorps) was assigned to Air Fleet 1.

It took von Leeb three more weeks to regroup his armies. In the meantime, the pressure of his left flank against the Soviet forces in Northern Estonia intensified. Overcoming stiff enemy resistance, the Germans slowly but steadily gained more ground. On 7 August the 18. Army of Generaloberst Georg von Küchler finally reached the Baltic coast. Thus, the Soviet front in Estonia was split in two: part of the Red force was pushed into a small foothold around Tallinn, while the rest was forced to retreat to the Narva River.

The German attack on Leningrad resumed only on 8-10 August, thereby giving the defenders of the city an extra three weeks to strengthen their positions. Right from the outset von Küchler's assault detachments encountered very stiff resistance. But they were made of seasoned troops that gradually gained the upper hand. The Red units cracked under their pressure and gave ground. Novgorod was abandoned on 15 August; Kingisepp fell the next day; Narva was lost on 17 August and finally Luga, the cornerstone of the Soviet defense, was evacuated on 19 August. Thus, in a matter of about ten days the bitterly held fortified belt was penetrated along its entire length. Worse still, on 20 August the German spearheads cut off the Moscow – Leningrad highway and railroad.

Meanwhile, a real drama was unfolding at Tallinn. Like Leningrad, the Estonian capital was not prepared to parry ground attacks from the south. Consequently about 25,000 local civilians were mobilized to dig trenches and anti-tank ditches at the approaches to the city. Ad-hoc units were created from marines, sailors and Baltic workers. These measures, however, worked only for a short period. The regular army troops, the naval infantrymen, the sailors and the communist militia were not able to withstand the heavy German pressure and during the night of 27/28 August the evacuation of the Soviet units began. Some 40,000 troops and civilians boarded on more than 200 vessels that were organized into several convoys. They sailed east, towards Kronstadt and Leningrad, under constant German aerial and artillery bombardment. The result was the bloodiest naval catastrophe since the battle of Lepanto: about 15,000 men and women drowned in the sea and 84 ships and boats were sunk. Nevertheless, twice that number succeeded in reaching their final destination, bringing ashore not only their passengers but also thousands of tons of precious equipment.

The struggle for Estonia, however, didn't end with the fall of Tallinn. There were still Soviet pockets of resistance in the west of the country and on the islands of the Moonsund archipelago. But they were more than that - Stalin used them as air bases to launch harassing air raids on Berlin. Even though these night raids caused little if any damage to the capital of the Third Reich (only eight raids were conducted with 3-12 Pe-8 heavy bombers in each raid), Hitler understandably wanted to get rid of this threat. The German infantry landed on the islands on 6 September, but it was not before 22 October that the defenders were finished off.

The last Soviet bastion at the entrance of Gulf of Finland, the naval base of Hanko, was evacuated by sea to Leningrad by 2 December. Once again the sneaking out came at heavy price: 20 vessels were lost and nearly 5,000 troops (out of 28,000) drowned in the sea.

* * *

The collapse of the Kingisepp – Luga position caused serious concern in the Soviet Supreme Command as to the ability of their troops to hold the Leningrad area. Wasting no time, a new task force, the Leningrad Front, was established, comprising of all the armies deployed in the vicinity of the city. It was entrusted to Lieutenant-General Markian Popov. Furthermore, two fresh armies were hurriedly deployed along the eastern bank of the Volkhov River, with the mission of preventing a deep German outflanking maneuver to the southeast.

Hopes were high that Popov at last would be able to halt von Leeb's onslaught but they didn't materialize and on 6 September he was replaced by one of Stalin's most trusted associates, Marshal Kliment Voroshilov. Two days later all rail connections and roads to the city were severed. But Leningrad did not fall immediately to Hitler's

Marshal Kliment Voroshilov was among Stalin's most trusted associates. He briefly commanded the Leningrad Front during the first half of September 1941. (NAC)

troops. Instead it resisted. Thus began one of the most brutal sieges in the history of mankind.

Nearly three million civilians and half a million troops found themselves trapped in the cauldron. The only way to feed them was either to move supplies across Lake Ladoga or to fly them in by transport planes. Stalin was well aware that the fall of the city that had been proclaimed the cradle of the Bolshevik Revolution would mean a catastrophe of epic proportions. That's why by 11 September 1941 he had sacked Voroshilov; Marshal Zhukov, an exceptionally brutal commander and one of Stalin's most trusted warlords, was appointed in his place.

In the meantime, the Germans penetrated into the suburbs. However, they were not able to break into the city itself owing to the determined Soviet resistance. They also failed to eliminate the so-called Oranienbaum Bridgehead, an isolated peninsula to the west of the city that would remain under Soviet control throughout the entire siege and would play a significant role in protecting Leningrad. The efforts of von Küchler's 18. Army were further hindered by the decision of its Finnish ally to stop at the 1939 Finnish-Soviet border, some 20 km from the northern suburbs of Leningrad.

It was apparent that the German offensive was not going as planned and Feldmarschall von Leeb was now under considerable pressure from Hitler to complete his assignment of encircling Leningrad, establishing contact with the Finns and eliminating the Soviet Baltic Fleet. The troops of Army Group 'North' were desperately needed at the Moscow front, where the German armed forces were preparing what was supposed to be the final offensive of the war. In spite of the sincere assurances from von Leeb that his divisions were still capable of making good progress, they could gain no more ground and were effectively halted by an impregnable belt of Soviet field fortifications.

Hitler could wait no longer and by 17 September shifted Panzer Group 4, which von Leeb considered to be his main striking force, from the outskirts of Leningrad to the Moscow front. Without the panzer group the whole dynamics of the German offensive in the north changed and taking the city by a direct assault was no longer an objective. Instead, Hitler ordered Leningrad to be besieged, raised to the ground by artillery and air force, and starved to death.

The artillery bombardment of Leningrad began in August 1941, when the Germans arrived within shelling distance of the city limits. Gradually, heavy caliber guns and siege mortars were placed along the southern perimeter. The pounding of the city continued with varying intensity for more than two years. It was very fierce during 1942 and was stepped up even further in 1943 when several times as many shells fell on the trapped city.

In contrast, the Luftwaffe strikes were very intense during September 1941, when the main city food store was destroyed, several hospitals were hit and the battleship 'Marat' was crippled. The German aerial activity gradually diminished during the following months. Nevertheless, the bombers and the artillery shells took a heavy toll on the inhabitants of Leningrad: by January 1944 nearly 6,000 of them had been killed while another 21,000 were wounded.

THE SOVIET RELIEF ATTEMPTS

There were two ways to sustain the siege of Leningrad: either to build a route for bringing a constant flow of supplies into the city or to lift the blockade by force.

The supply route was established in November 1941 over the southern part of Lake Ladoga and the Soviet-controlled land corridor between the lake and Leningrad. It quickly became known as 'The Road of Life'. The transportation of supplies across Ladoga was achieved by trucks driven over the thick ice in the winter months and by boats during the warmer months. They also were used to evacuate civilians from the besieged city, especially children. The protection of 'The Road of Life' was provided by vessels of the Ladoga Flotilla, by the AA guns and fighter planes of the Leningrad PVO Corps, and by the route security troops.

Needless to say, any trip on the 45-km-long 'Road of Life' was a very dangerous undertaking not only because there was the risk of vehicles sinking through broken ice, but also because it was constantly bombarded by the Germans. (During the summer and the autumn of 1942 the German counter-supply operations were supported by Naval Detachment 'K', a combined Finnish-German-Italian unit comprising four Italian boats, four German minelayers and a Finnish torpedo boat. Despite sinking some small Soviet vessels, their operations in the shallow lake were, on the whole, a failure.)

* * *

The first Soviet relief attempt was launched literally a couple of days after the land communications to the city had been severed. On 10 September 1941, the independent 54th Army of Marshal Kulik attacked in the area south of Ladoga from the east, along the southern shore of the lake. The repeated Soviet attempts to reach Sinyavino, Mga and Shlisselburg collapsed in the face of the very determined German resistance. Worse still, the poorly armed attackers sustained bloody losses (more than 10,000 men). By 26 September the offensive, which would go down in history as the 1st Sinyavino Operation, was called off and Kulik himself was relieved of command.

The Leningrad Front also made an attempt to establish contact with the relief force by attacking across the Neva River to the east. The actions of the so-called 'Neva Operational Group' of General Pshennikov were also a total failure. Its only success was the securing of the so-called Nevsky Pyatachok, a miniature bridgehead measuring 1 by 1.5 km, on the eastern bank of the Neva. The struggle for this foothold would continue till 29 April 1942 when it was finally eliminated by the Germans.

Zhukov was very enraged by the failure of the Neva Operational Group to gain significant ground and sacked General Pshennikov. Shortly afterwards the Marshal himself was flown out of the besieged city, too, because a highly critical situation had arisen at the gates of Moscow where the main Soviet forces were about to be annihilated and a strong-willed officer was needed to save the capital. Major-General Fedyuninsky was appointed acting commander of the Leningrad Front.

Even though unsuccessful, the 1st Sinyavino Operation was a ringing alarm bell for von Leeb and his staff. The bottleneck-like corridor to the south of Ladoga, which was now the responsibility of Generaloberst Ernst Busch's 16. Army, was considerably

The Road of Life, winter of 1942. (RinP)

reinforced and several new divisions were urgently brought there. Among them was the elite 7. Fallschirmjäger-Division, whose paratroopers were transported by planes, and the Spanish 'Blue' Division that had been formally incorporated into the Wehrmacht as the 250. Infanterie-Division. The latter was a very interesting formation that numbered about 18,000 men, nearly all of them Spaniards with membership in the Falange Fascist Party, as well as a small number of Portuguese.

The 2nd Sinyavino Operation was launched on 20 October 1941. This time the actions of both forces were more coordinated since the armies operating on the outer front (54th and 55th) had been placed under the Leningrad Front. Nevertheless, the unified chain of command didn't help and the Soviets once again gained very little ground at the cost of bloody losses (the bayonet strength of some of the rifle regiments fell below 300 men). By the end of the month the offensives of both the Neva Operational Group and the task force attacking from the east (i.e. 54th and 55th Armies) were brought to a standstill. Fedyuninsky felt he was underqualified for the position and asked Moscow to allow him to swap places with the commander of the 54th Army. Stavka (the Soviet Supreme Command) fulfilled his request and by 27 October Khozin was already in command of the entire Leningrad Front.

The 2nd Sinyavino Operation was overshadowed by the events at Tikhvin, where the Germans at first were very successful. The onslaught of Busch's 16. Army began on 16 October 1941, when the Volkohov River was crossed north of Chudovo. Its objective was, by carrying out a wide outflanking maneuver, to establish contact with the Finnish forces advancing through Karelia, thereby closing a double ring around Leningrad.The army's spearhead, the XXXIX Panzer Corps, captured Tikhvin by 9 November, but then the weather deteriorated; the temperature fell way below freezing point and this, combined with mounting losses and the increasing enemy counterattacks, brought Busch's offensive to a standstill. Then Stalin sent more reserves to the endangered area and the Soviets went over to the counterattack. The diminishing German forces, which were totally unprepared for winter warfare, abandoned the town on 9 December. By Christmas Day of 1941 they had already evacuated the entire corridor and had pulled back beyond the Volkhov.

* * *

By the end of November 1941 the Nazi offensive everywhere on the Eastern Front had run out of steam. The German troops could advance only along the few hard-surface roads and the Luftwaffe was operating from a limited number of improvised forward airfields. The snow and cold were everywhere. The engines of vehicles and airplanes had to be heated for hours before starting them. It was apparent that the Wehrmacht and its allies were overextended, exhausted and poorly equipped for winter. The initiative gradually passed to the Soviets, and Stalin and the Stavka decided that the moment had come to launch decisive counterattacks to push the invaders away from the capital.

The Soviet winter counteroffensive began on 5 December 1941. At first, the limited Red attacks were successful and within weeks they were upgraded into far more extensive and ambitious operations undertaken by literally all Soviet fronts deployed between Leningrad and the Black Sea. They were, however, hastily planned and poorly executed, and at no point achieved the objectives assigned to them. Worse still, on several occasions attacking Soviet armies were trapped by the Germans in the forested marshy areas of central and northern Russia, and subsequently annihilated. Sometimes these cauldron battles lasted weeks, but sometimes it took the Wehrmacht months to mop up the last remaining pockets of resistance. Most dramatic was the fate of the 2nd Shock Army, whose struggle for survival lasted nearly half a year.

* * *

By mid-December 1941 the Soviet forces operating to the east of Leningrad (54th Army, 4th and 52nd Independent Armies and the Novgorod Operational Group) were not under unified command and despite their success at Tikhvin their actions were still poorly coordinated. In order to provide the troops deployed east of the Volkhov River with better leadership, on 17 December 1941 the Stavka assembled them (save for the northernmost 54th Army) into a separate task force, the Volkhov Front, under Army-General Meretskov. It was also immediately reinforced with two fresh armies (2nd Shock and 59th).

On 7 January 1942 Stalin, who was convinced that the freezing German troops were on the point of exhaustion, ordered an all-out offensive along the entire Eastern Front. In the north his ambitions were to destroy a sizeable part of Army Group 'North' by striking the enemy positions between Staraya Russa and Leningrad. Von Küchler's 18. Army, in particular, was to be cut off around Leningrad by a bold strike from the southeast delivered by the fresh 2nd Shock Army.

The offensive of 2nd Shock Army commenced on 7 January 1942 exactly at the point where the Germans had launched their drive on Tikhvin three months earlier. The Volkhov was crossed and the defensive lines of the 18. Army were breached on a

30 km frontage. Soviet spearheads penetrated 70–74 km deep inside the German rear area. The other Soviet armies, however, failed to provide the required support, even though the offensive was planned as a combined operation between the Volkhov and Leningrad Fronts. (They were supposed to take part in the later stages, at scheduled intervals.) Before long the 2nd Shock Army became stranded.

When planning the operation Stalin and his aides, apparently, had failed to realize how poorly equipped, undertrained and under-gunned the 2nd Shock Army was. It had very few tanks and many of the newly produced guns were missing sights (though they were urgently delivered by plane in the course of the battle}. The forces of the army were also dispersed and poorly supplied. Worse still, it was led by a very incompetent commander, a certain Lieutenant-General Sokolov, who was an NKVD commissar and a former deputy of the notorious Lavrentiy Beria, the head of NKVD.

Shortly after the beginning of the offensive, Meretskov convinced the Stavka to get rid of the useless Sokolov. He was replaced by Lieutenant-General Klykov, but the change in the command didn't reflect on the situation on the battlefield. In mid-March German counterattacks isolated and encircled the unfortunate army. In mid-April 1942, Klykov got ill and had to be flown out of the pocket. He was succeeded by Lieutenant-General Andrey Vlasov, who had been sent a month before from Moscow to become Meretskov's deputy after displaying splendid leadership skills in the Moscow winter counteroffensive. But the situation was already beyond repair. Throughout the three months of brutal fighting in atrocious conditions, the 2nd Shock Army was neither relieved nor able to break out. Finally, in the last week of June 1942, the Germans delivered their final blow and fully annihilated it. About 33,000 prisoners were taken. Among them was General Vlasov himself, who later cooperated with the German authorities to raise the 'Russian Liberation Army' and was labeled an arch-traitor by the Soviet propaganda.

* * *

The next Soviet attempt to lift the siege took place in late August 1942. By then important changes had occurred in the command chains of both belligerents: Lieutenant-General Govorov had replaced Khozin as commander of the Leningrad Front in late June 1942, while von Küchler had been appointed in place of von Leeb in January 1942. Georg Lindemann, one of Küchler's corps commanders, took over the 18. Army.

Feldmarschall Georg von Küchler decorates Stabsfeldwebel Georg Jura of 28. Jäger-Division with Knight's Cross for his exceptional bravery displayed in the winter battle at Lake Ladoga, 28 April 1943. Von Küchler was commander of Army Group 'North' from 17 January 1942 to 31 January 1944 when he was succeeded by Generaloberst Walther Model. (NAC)

The plan of the new Sinyavino Offensive didn't differ much from the ill-fated 1st and 2nd Sinyavino Operations of late-1941. It called for two powerful task forces (the Leningrad and Volkhov Fronts) to attack towards each other from the west and east respectively, in the general direction of Sinyavino where they were supposed to meet. Thus, the so-called Mga bottleneck (i.e. the German-controlled penetration corridor to the east of the Neva) would be eliminated and land communications between Leningrad and the mainland restored.

The Soviets, however, didn't know that the Germans had just completed their own offensive plans for a final assault on the besieged city, Operation 'Nordlicht' ('Northern Light'). The main objective of the operation was to capture Leningrad, thus bringing to an end the siege and freeing hundreds of thousands of troops. Von Küchler was lacking the proper forces to storm the city and for that purpose the 11. Army (five divisions) was transferred from Crimea. Hitler firmly believed that the commander of that army, Feldmarschall Erich von Manstein, was the right man for the job because he and his four divisions had the reputation of being 'siege experts' and therefore possessed the experience for taking heavily fortified places (Manstein had just captured Sevastopol after a several-months-long siege). The army was also to receive siege artillery of the 'Dora' and 'Karl' type, as well as newly manufactured Tiger tanks that hadn't seen their baptism of fire so far.

The Germans were unaware of the Soviet preparations and when Govorov struck first on 19 August, they were caught completely by surprise. Meretskov's Volkhov Front delivered the main blow on 27 August. The 223. Infanterie-Division, which had just arrived from France, was unable to withstand the onslaught and disintegrated. The Soviet tanks and infantry rapidly approached the Sinyavino heights.

With the Germans in dire straits, Feldmarschall von Manstein, who had arrived on the same day in the Leningrad area, was urgently called to save the situation. From 28 August he began shifting the forces of the 11. Army which were assembling for 'Northern Light' in the Mga bottleneck. Even though the initial German counterattacks were not very successful, they gradually began to halt the Soviet drive. Meretskov's forces could gain no more ground and temporary switched over to the defensive. A ten-day stalemate followed during which Manstein's army was significantly reinforced. Then, on 21 September, the Germans launched a decisive counterattack against the shoulders of the Soviet penetration corridor, striking simultaneously from the north and south. Their efforts were supported by tanks, massive artillery bombardments and dive bombers. After five days of heavy fighting, the German divisions linked up and cut off the bulge formed by the Soviet forces. The bulk of Meretskov's task force (the 8th Army and the reconstituted 2nd Shock Army) found itself caught in a deadly trap. There was no way out even though the heavy fighting east of Sinyavino continued till 15 October when the last pockets of resistance were finally mopped up.

Even though at least part of Meretskov's task force, as well as many small groups and individual soldiers, broke out the Soviet losses were considerable. The Germans claimed about 12,000 prisoners, 244 tanks, more than 300 artillery pieces and 500 mortars. The total losses of both Soviet fronts amounted to more than 113,000 men killed, wounded and missing.

It was apparent that the Sinyavino Offensive was a failure, but it caused the Germans to transfer the forces intended for 'Northern Light' to the endangered sector. The resulting attrition meant that the Wehrmacht could not execute the planned assault on Leningrad and the operation was put on hold. In November 1942, the staff of the 11. Army was relocated to Vitebsk. Thus, 'Northern Light' was canceled for good and the Germans were never again able to launch an offensive against Leningrad.

* * *

In 1943 the encirclement of Leningrad was finally broken. In the morning of 12 January 1943 the Soviets launched Operation 'Iskra' ('Spark'), following the usual heavy artillery preparation. After some very heavy fighting, the Red Army forces overcame the resolute defense of the German troops guarding both sides of the Mga bottleneck. On 18 January the spearhead of Volkhov Front (372nd Rifle Division) established contact at Workers Settlement No. 1 with the forces of the Leningrad Front advancing from the west (123rd Rifle Division). Thus, they opened a 10-12 km wide land corridor and at last provided some relief to the troubled inhabitants of the city. Wasting no time, on the same day the GKO (Soviet Defense State Committee) ordered a railway linking Leningrad with the rest of the country to be urgently constructed through the recaptured corridor. It was finished ahead of any schedules and the first trains loaded with supplies arrived in the city on 6 February 1943.

Operation 'Iskra' officially ended on 30 January 1943. It was a strategic victory for the Soviets. First and foremost, the success of the Red Army eliminated the slightest possibility of the capture of the city by the Germans and of a German–Finnish link up as Govorov's Leningrad Front was now very well supplied, could receive substantial reinforcements and was able to co-operate more closely with Meretskov's Volkhov Front. Establishing the land corridor also meant that the civilian population would receive more food and more people could be safely evacuated from the city. The lifting of the siege also had a significant psychological and political effect. It coincided with Soviet victories at Stalingrad and in the Caucasus and so strengthened both the confidence of the Soviet people and relations within the Allied coalition while at the same time increasing the pressure on the members of the Axis camp.

Needless to say, Stalin was very pleased by the success. Already on 18 January Zhukov, who coordinated the actions of both fronts as a Stavka representative, was promoted to rank of Marshal of The Soviet Union. Both Govorov and Meretskov were awarded the Order of Suvorov 1st Class. In addition, Govorov was promoted to Colonel-General.

However, despite the lifting of the siege, Stalin and the Stavka knew that Operation 'Iskra' was incomplete as the corridor opened by Govorov and Meretskov was quite narrow and was still in range of German artillery. Furthermore, the tactically important heights at Sinyavino, as well as the village itself (which had been transformed into a stronghold) were still in German hands. There was some unfinished business to the west of Leningrad, too, where the Oranienbaum Bridgehead was still isolated from the city. All this led the Soviet High Command to develop a plan for a much more ambitious operation codenamed 'Polyarnaya Zvezda' ('Polar Star'). It was similar in scope to the failed offensive of the 2nd Shock Army during the previous winter. Its objective was, by launching a pincer attack from the vicinity of Lake Ilmen to the northwest, to cut off German forces deployed within the Leningrad salient, i.e. most of Army Group 'North'.

In order to meet the ambitions new objectives assigned to them, from 10 February to 2 April 1943 the Soviet forces opposing von Küchler's army group launched a series of local operations along the entire perimeter but gained very little ground. It was a very costly failure since the three fronts involved in 'Polar Star' (i.e. the Leningrad, Volkhov and North-Western Fronts) sustained heavy losses: about 280,000 men were killed, wounded and missing.

In the vicinity of Leningrad, in particular, two such operations were launched. They were aimed at the Mga and Sinyavino, which were attacked from the north, as well as against the western shoulder of the Mga bottleneck, which was attacked in the vicinity of Krasny Bor. Only in the latter sector did the Leningrad Front achieve some success by advancing 10-15 km to the southeast, in the general direction of Tosno. The Soviet breakthrough was prevented by the very determined resistance put up by SS-Polizei-Division, the Spanish 'Blue' Division and the 'international' 2. SS-Infanterie-Brigade.

Oberstleutnant Franz Griesbach, commander of Grenadier-Regiment 399 of 170. Infanterie-Division. Griesbach especially distinguished himself during the second Battle of Lake Ladoga in January 1943. This earned him the Knight's Cross with Oak Leaves and promotion to Oberst. On 15 February 1944 he was appointed commander of 170. Infanterie-Division. (NAC)

* * *

The Soviet attempts to crush the reminder of the Mga bottleneck and capture Sinyavino resumed in the summer of 1943. On 22 July, the so called '3rd Ladoga Battle' erupted which lasted roughly a month. It brought no success to the attackers (the 67th Army), even though they were now more powerful than ever. In mid-September the army renewed its attempts to seize the Sinyavino heights, but once again was beaten back.

The 1943 spring and summer battles left Lindemann's 18. Army overstretched and very exhausted. The loss of the strategic initiative and the lack of sufficient reinforcements convinced the command of Army Group 'North' to shorten the front line by evacuating certain sectors that could potentially be used by the enemy to encircle a large number of German forces.

One such sector was the Kirishi bridgehead on the eastern bank of the Volkhov, just to the northeast of Chudovo. The withdrawal began on 2 October with the troops retreating step by step to occupy a well-prepared shortened position further

Generaloberst Georg Lindemann (left) and a regimental commander move through a destroyed forest during an inspection of units positioned south of Lake Ladoga, October 1943. (The photo was taken in the aftermath of the Third Battle of Ladoga.) Lindemann took the command of 18. Army on 16 January 1942. In the summer of the same year, he was promoted to Generaloberst. He led the 18. Army throughout the campaigns around Leningrad and during the January 1944 retreat from the Oranienbaum bridgehead to Narva. He was promoted to commander of Army Group 'North' on 31 March 1944. On 4 July 1944 he was relieved and replaced by Generaloberst Friessner. (NAC)

in the rear, on the western bank of the river. The Soviets (the 54th Army of Volkhov Front) immediately began to pursue them in an attempt to exploit the situation. The Germans, however, were prepared for such an eventuality and repelled all enemy attacks. The Soviet attempts to breach the positions of the 96. Infanterie-Division continued till the middle of the month but failed to bring the desired results.

The evacuation of the Kirishi bridgehead and regrouping in some other sectors allowed Lindemann during October and November 1943 to free six of his most experienced infanterie-divisions, as well as the elite 5. Gebirgsjäger-Division. The 18. Army, however, was not allowed to keep them in the second echelon as tactical reserves. Because of the critical situation on the southern flank of the army group, as well as in the other sectors of the Eastern Front, these divisions went to more important battlefields.

Soviet soldiers inspect a blown-up Tiger of schwere Panzer-Abteilung 502, January 1944. (author's collection)

In October, the 18. Army sustained yet another heavy blow: the 'Blue' Division was pulled out of the front and sent back to Spain for political reasons. It was a very reliable formation that had proved itself in many battles and had earned the respect of both friend and foe. From September 1941 to October 1943 more than 45,000 Spanish soldiers (volunteers and conscripts) served on the Eastern Front through rotation. Nearly 4,000 of them were killed (including 153 officers) and another 13,000 wounded while those missing in action accounted for a further 300 men.

The troops that remained at the gates of Leningrad were not of the same quality as those that had reached the outskirts of the city in September 1941. Some of them were battle-hardened veterans but others were nothing but cannon fodder. Among the latter were six Luftwaffe field divisions that were relatively well-equipped but undertrained and lacked combat experience.

Even the armored units that arrived as reinforcements were not of sufficient quality. For example, on 2 November 1943 an order was issued by Colonel-General Guderian, who was General-Inspector of the panzer troops at the time, to transfer to the Leningrad area 60 disabled Ausf. D Panther tanks. They were mechanically unreliable and had to be used as fixed anti-tank weapons. A special unit was formed for the purpose, which received the official designation Panzer-Abteilung (bo.) 'Nord'. The personnel that had to man the stranded tanks were drawn from I./Panzer-Regiment 29, whose training had just been completed. Upon the arrival at the front, the men of the battalion (three companies) realized that some of the tanks could be repaired and gradually brought them back to life. Thus, much to his surprise, Lindemann got a panzer unit although it was mechanically not very fit for combat. The immobile tanks that could not be fixed remained with the frontline divisions.

Given the above it is not surprising that by the summer of 1943 the German High Command began to build a fall-back defensive position called the 'Panther' Line along the 1939 border between the USSR and the Baltic States. Hitler was about to sanction the withdrawal of Army Group 'North' to the 'Panther' Line in late autumn 1943 but changed his mind and ordered the 16. and 18. Armies to stay where they were, fearing that otherwise Finland might decide to leave the war.

CHAPTER 2

THE LENINGRAD–NOVGOROD OFFENSIVE, JANUARY 1944

PLANNING AND PREPARATIONS

In 1941-43 the Red Army launched several operations to break the siege of Leningrad, but none of them were completely successful. The cradle of the Bolshevik Revolution had been under siege for more than two years and, as was already mentioned, till January 1943 had to rely on a fragile ice road over Lake Ladoga ('the Road of Life') for delivery of supplies. Even though in January 1943 the Red Army was able to open a narrow land corridor to the city, it became an easy target for the German artillery. Worse still, even though the Leningrad Front had established a centralized counter-battery organization that began pin-pointing and silencing the German long-range guns, Lindemann's 18. Army kept shelling the city at frequent intervals. Given the above, it was clear that the threat to the city could only be eliminated by pushing Army Group 'North' away from Leningrad.

Planning for the offensive that would liberate the Leningrad area from the Germans began in early September 1943. Two plans, codenamed 'Neva 1' and 'Neva 2', were developed. The former was to be put in effect if Army Group 'North' withdrew its divisions from the vicinity of the city on its own initiative or on orders from above in order to reinforce strategically more important areas, such as Central Russia or the Ukraine. It should be noted here that both the Stavka and the leadership of the Leningrad Front believed this was possible, let alone that Hitler considered such a scenario, too.

The latter plan, 'Neva 2', was to be implemented if the Germans didn't withdraw from the Leningrad area within the following months. It called for a three-pronged offensive that would be launched simultaneously from the Oranienbaum Bridgehead, the Pulkovo Heights (the southern defensive perimeter of Leningrad) and from the vicinity of Novgorod. The ultimate objective was to encircle the German 18. Army in a Stalingrad-like pocket and subsequently destroy it in the swampy forested area south of Leningrad. In the meantime, the 2nd Baltic Front was to attack the right flank of Army Group 'North' at Nevel, thereby preventing the 16. Army from transferring troops to the Leningrad-Novgorod area. The onslaught was planned to begin in the winter, when sufficient number of troops and materiel could be moved over frozen ground without much difficulty.

Fortunately for Stalin, Finland had ruled out any form of participation in a direct attack on Leningrad already in 1941. Thus, any threat to the city from the north had been eliminated a priori. This, together with the withdrawal in the autumn of 1943 of several seasoned divisions sent to stabilize the crumbling fronts further south, made Lindemann's 18. Army very vulnerable by the beginning of 1944.

* * *

The preparations for the 'Neva 2', which was officially redesignated 'January Thunder', started in early November 1943. Shortly afterwards the ice gradually began to close in on the Gulf of Finland and Lake Ladoga. The Soviets immediately took measures to reinforce the Oranienbaum Bridgehead, which was now considered one of their principal jump-off points. The staff of the recently reconstituted 2nd Shock Army was relocated there, followed by four rifle divisions and several artillery, engineer and tank units. They were transferred to the foothold on night convoys of barges and small vessels that were escorted by patrol boats and minesweepers. In this way no less than 30,000 troops, 47 tanks, 400 artillery pieces, 1,400 trucks and more than 10,000 tons of ammunition were shipped to Oranienbaum. Apart from that, some forces and supplies arrived by transport planes, as well as by trucks (in early January 1944 from Kronstadt, over the frozen Gulf of Finland). The Germans repeatedly attempted to disrupt the buildup by shelling the convoys, but not a single boat was lost in the process.

After Lake Ladoga froze, the main body of the Leningrad Front was also reinforced in a similar fashion: about 22,000 men, 140 tanks, 380 artillery pieces and some 800 trucks were sent overland to the city. This allowed Govorov, who had just been promoted to the rank of Army-General, to considerably strengthen his formations deployed along the southern perimeter of Leningrad.

By mid-January 1944 the four armies of the Leningrad Front comprised 33 rifle divisions, 3 rifle brigades and 5 fortified regions. They were deployed on a frontage of 256 km, which gave Govorov an average density of one division per 6.5 km. Furthermore, since the quiet sectors were stripped of troops, the Soviets achieved much higher densities in the critical breakthrough zones. All of the available armored forces (four tank brigades, nine tank regiments and three self-propelled artillery regiments) and about 80% of the artillery were assigned to the armies that would deliver the main blows: the 2nd Shock and the 42nd.

The three armies of Volkhov Front consisted of 22 rifle divisions, 6 rifle brigades and 2 fortified regions deployed on a frontage of 232 km (i.e. roughly one division per every 9 km). Since the front had to deliver its main blow at a single point (Novgorod), Army-General Meretskov assembled most of the resources placed at his disposal in the sector of the 59th Army, including half of the artillery and nearly all the tanks.

By the beginning of the offensive both fronts were not only well-trained and pretty well supplied, but also numerically very strong. They numbered about 882,000 men (374,500 of them were in the rifle divisions), more than 6,500 artillery pieces, 7,756 mortars, and 1,238 tanks and self-propelled guns. They were supported from the air by about 1,100 aircraft of 13th and 14th Air Armies.

* * *

As mentioned earlier, Lindemann's 18. Army ended 1943 in a much reduced strength – by 26 December it numbered 19 divisions, 2 brigades and a divisional battle group. To make matters worse, by the beginning of the Soviet onslaught two more divisions (96. and 254.) had been urgently transferred to the Ukraine. Thus, only seventeen and half German divisions, and two SS brigades were destined to meet the onslaught of the two Soviet fronts.

The strongest of them was perhaps the 11. SS-Panzergrenadier-Division 'Nordland', which had arrived from the Balkans in late 1943 together with its sister formation the 4. SS-Panzergrenadier-Brigade 'Nederland'. Both were placed under the III. SS-Panzer-Corps of Obergruppenführer Felix Steiner.

One of the most pervasive myths surrounding both formations is that they were made almost exclusively of foreign (non-German) volunteers of Germanic origin: Norwegians, Danes, Swedes, Dutchmen and so on. In reality, by the autumn of 1943 only about 2,000 of the 'Nordland' troops had come from the 'Nordic' countries while the rest were Germans, mainly Volksdeutsche from the Banat region in southwestern Rumania. Brigade 'Nederland' was more ethnically homogeneous (about 60% of its rank and file were Dutchmen), but, at the same time, it was much smaller in size.

The III. SS-Panzer-Corps occupied the Oranienbaum Bridgehead, one of the four principal defensive sectors of the 18. Army. A solid defensive line was built there with the aim of preventing the Russians from breaking out of the bridgehead. Apart from the SS men, it was also occupied by two so-called Luftwaffe field divisions (9. and 10.) which had very little combat value. The corps possessed several heavy artillery units, 96 anti-tank guns and even its own armored reserve – the already mentioned I./Panzer-Regiment 29 that had very few Panthers in running condition.

Leningrad was besieged from the south by two army corps (L. and LIV.) with six infantry--divisions between them. Their grenadiers manned relatively well-developed defensive positions and could count on the support of a considerable number of anti-tank guns (197).

The tactically very important Sinyavino heights (the lower part of the former Mga 'bottleneck') was third principal defensive sector controlled by the 18. Army.

Here, Generaloberst Lindemann had deployed the XXVI. Army Corps with only two infanterie-divisions that were supported by 39 anti-tank guns. Apparently, Lindemann didn't expect miracles from them because in the rear zone a switch position had been constructed, the so-called Rollbahn-Stellung. It ran along the Leningrad–Moscow railroad and motorway and was meant not only to protect the main communication arteries, but also to provide the defenders with means for disengagement and fighting withdrawal.

The fourth principal defensive sector was the frontline along the Volkhov River. It was held by two army corps (XXVIII. and XXXVIII.) with just six divisions between them, half of which were nearly useless Luftwaffe field formations. There was no doubt that the troops occupying it were by no means sufficient to hold the entire perimeter, that's why Lindemann decided to construct the most solid field fortifications on its southern flank, in the vicinity of Novgorod. The two corps commanders could count on total of 104 anti-tank guns. Right from the outset it was clear that their number was quite insignificant and forming effective anti-tank barriers was simply out of question.

The very reliable 61. Infanterie-Division, which was deployed at Leningrad, was the sole tactical reserve of the 18. Army.

* * *

It is worth noting that the above-mentioned defensive positions were not some meaningless pencil lines on maps. A great deal of effort was made on the part of the German command to build them. In 1943 a total of 90,000 enlisted personnel and 3,100 'volunteers' were employed to construct field fortifications in those sectors. As result of this, by the beginning of the Soviet offensive, 122 km of trenches and 27.6 km of anti tank ditches had been dug, 151.3 km of barbed wire were strung and 4,828 firing points were set up.

Even more attention was paid to the 'Panther' Line, a fall-back defensive position running along the 1939 border between the USSR and the Baltic States. It was completed under the command of Generalmajor Erich Abberger, the senior engineer officer of Army Group 'North', and his staff of specialists. There was no doubt that Abberger was the best man for the job, since he had been responsible for the design of most of the line of defenses that had contained the Soviets at Novgorod for more than two years. Apart from that, he and his aides had learned to deal with the nightmarish terrain and road conditions then prevailing in that part of Russia.

The total length of the 'Panther' Line was about 500 km. More than 30% of it (a sector ca. 160 km long) was protected by Lake Peipus. The rest of it was divided into sub-sectors that were provided with building material in accordance with their technical and tactical importance.

The actual construction of the 'Panther' Line began on 7 September 1943, immediately after the determination of its course on the terrain. The most essential part of the work was completed by the end of December 1943. However, the remainder was finished only by the beginning of March 1944 when the positions were occupied by the retreating German troops.

The erection of such an ambitious defensive line was a labor-intensive job. To give an example, from 7 October to 31 December 1943 the following installations were constructed in the 'Panther' Line:

- Anti-tank obstacles: 37 km
- Barbed wire entanglements: 250 km
- Firing points (emplacements for machineguns, anti-tank guns, etc.): 1,345 km
- Shelters: 5,460 km
- Concrete shelters: 645 km
- Steel shelters: 75 km

In addition, 30 km of roads and 1,160 road bridges had been constructed during the period in question. Apart from that, by 1 January 1944, the construction of 380 km of barbed wire entanglements, 100 km of firing points, 3,000 km of shelters, 180 km of shelters, 40 km of steel shelters, 30 km of roads and 2,100 road bridges was still in progress.

* * *

The 18. Army was to receive close support from Air Fleet 1, whose units at that moment had less than 300 combat aircraft. This guaranteed the Soviets at least three-fold superiority in the air. 'Stalin's Falcons' were prepared to face very stiff opposition but, much to their amazement, throughout the whole of January the Luftwaffe was nowhere to be seen. Due to unknown reasons, during the final battle at the gates of Leningrad the activity of the German pilots was limited to sporadic aerial attacks carried out by small groups of planes or by individual machines and reconnaissance missions.

'JANUARY THUNDER'

On 14 January the 2nd Shock Army went over to the offensive from the Oranienbaum Bridgehead with two rifle corps. The army was now led by a new commander, Lieutenant-General Fedyuninsky, who, as we recall, briefly led the Leningrad Front in the autumn of 1941. The assault was preceded by the usual powerful artillery preparation. Furthermore, 'Stalin's Falcons' hit the German strongpoints hard. At the same time, the combat engineers cleared passages in the minefields and barbed-wire entanglements.

Despite all these support measures, the Soviet infantry advanced very little. Skillfully using the well-built field fortifications, the troops of SS-Obergruppenführer Felix Steiner offered fierce resistance and counterattacked at every opportunity. Displaying courage and skill, the SS troops and the soldiers of the Luftwaffe field divisions almost brought Fedyuninsky's offensive to a standstill. The situation remained unchanged during the following two days: the Russians attacked with vigor, the Germans, the Dutchmen and the Scandinavians fired back relentlessly and repeatedly counterattacked.

The 42nd Army joined 'January Thunder' on 15 January. The three rifle corps of Colonel-General Maslennikov attacked from the Pulkovo Heights, in the southwest of Leningrad, to the west, towards the spearheads of the 2nd Shock Army. They encountered the same troubles as Fedyuninsky's combat teams. Worse still, the armies armored units got stranded in the dense web of minefields and anti-tank ditches, and were unable to render proper support to the friendly infantry. Many tanks were put out of action by the precise fire of the German artillery.

* * *

By 16-17 January both armies had advanced no more than 10 km toward each other. Neither the 2nd Shock Army, nor the 42nd Army had any serious previous experience in breaching solid fortified positions. Nevertheless, by the end of Day 3 the Soviets succeeded in penetrating the main German line of resistance on a frontage of up to 23 km. This created good conditions for exploiting the initial success. Wasting no time, Fedyuninsky formed a mobile group consisting of the 152nd Tank Brigade and several infantry and artillery units and ordered it to take Ropsha. General Maslennikov, the commander of 42nd Army did the same, although his mobile group had much more armor: namely the 1st and 220th Tank Brigades and two self-propelled artillery regiments. Its mission was to take Krasnoe Selo and its vicinity.

The Germans began to lose their staying power. It was clear that Steiner's corps would not be able to hold out for very long. All tactical reserves, including the main one – the 61. Infanterie-Division – already had been thrown into the battle. But this didn't help the defenders to turn the tables in their favor. Now they were under threat of encirclement in the vicinity of their main strongpoints, Ropsha and Krasnoe Selo. Feldmarschall von Küchler had no other choice but to pull the XXVI. Army Corps out of the Mga bottleneck, thereby avoiding a disaster.

On 19 January the mobile groups of the 2nd Shock Army and the 42nd Army attacked Ropsha and Krasnoe Selo respectively. Shortly afterwards they established contact, thereby closing the ring around Steiner's corps. But the Soviet line had too many gaps in it and the Germans managed to breakout. They left behind a considerable

Lieutenant-General Ivan Fedyuninsky, the commander of 2nd Shock Army. (TsAMO)

number of heavy weapons and equipment, including 265 artillery pieces. On the next day, the remnants of the splinter groups that had failed to escape were finished off. The new frontline was now some 25 km away from the city which was now out of the effective range of the German artillery.

A German heavy artillery piece captured by 42nd Army in January 1944 at Krasnoye Selo, just southwest of Leningrad. (Georgy Lukin collection)

The 220-mm ammunition of the German battery captured by 42nd Army in Krasnoye Selo on 21 January 1944. (Georgy Lukin collection)

A four-gun German battery captured by 42nd Army in Krasnoye Selo on 21 January 1944. (Georgy Lukin collection)

A four-gun German battery captured by 42nd Army in Krasnoye Selo on 21 January 1944. (Georgy Lukin collection)

A StuG III assault gun of 18. Army destroyed in the vicinity of Khannolovo, not far from the southwestern suburbs of Leningrad, January 1944. (Georgy Lukin collection)

The German command forestalled these plans by pulling out its forces from the endangered sector. The 67th and 8th Armies went over to the offensive on 21 January, immediately upon detecting the withdrawal of the German divisions from the Mga bottleneck. They succeeded in capturing Mga and occupying the Murmansk railway line. But the chance to inflict an ultimate defeat on the enemy had gone since the Germans had already retreated in an orderly fashion and were now occupying a new line of resistance along the railway.

The sudden withdrawal of the German divisions from the Mga bottleneck forced the leadership of the Leningrad Front to rethink their plans. Govorov gave a new assignment to the 2nd Shock Army and 42nd Army: to capture Krasnogvardeysk and then to attack towards Kingisepp and Narva. In other words, instead of attacking southwards, now both armies were redirected to the southwest. They were to be supported by the 67th Army, which was ordered to evict the Germans from their position along the Leningrad–Moscow railway line.

The heavy fighting for the railroad, as well as for Krasnogvardeysk and Pushkin, which had been converted into strongpoints, lasted several days. The Germans tried to hold Krasnogvardeysk at any cost. Pressed by Hitler's usual 'no retreat' orders, von Küchler transferred his last tactical reserves to the area.

Pushkin was taken on 24 January. The all-out assault on Krasnogvardeysk began the following day. The brutal close-quarter battle continued till 26 January, when the town was finally captured by the Soviets. Thus, the continuous frontline of the 18. Army was fragmented; the badly battered German divisions retreated in a great hurry. In close pursuit of the retreating enemy, on 30 January the 2nd Shock Army reached the Luga River. But the men of Lieutenant-General Fedyuninsky didn't stop there and during the night of 31 January/1 February captured Kingisepp by a direct assault.

Thus, the troops of the Volkhov and Leningrad Fronts, in close cooperation with the Red Banner Baltic Fleet, put to an end the 900-day-long siege of Leningrad. A solid fortified line was breached, the German 18. Army sustained a heavy defeat. To honor these units, on 27 January both Moscow and Leningrad fired salutes of 24 salvoes from 324 guns.

The defeat of the III. SS-Panzer-Corps and the offensive of Volkhov Front, which had also started on 14 January, created good opportunities for a rapid advance in the rear zone of Army Group 'North'. That's why Govorov ordered the 42nd Army to shift its axis of advance to the south and attack in the direction of Krasnogvardeysk, Pushkin and Tosno. In so doing the army of Colonel-General Maslennikov was to cut off the communications of the German forces still holding the bulge east/southeast of Leningrad (XXVI. and XXVIII. Army Corps). Subsequently, they had to be destroyed in close cooperation with the 67th Army and the Volkhov Front. The ultimate objective of this new attack was to occupy the Leningrad–Moscow railway line and in so doing completely remove any threat to the 'Cradle of the Bolshevik Revolution'. Fedyuninsky's 2nd Shock Army was to lend a helping hand by outflanking Krasnogvardeysk to the southwest.

A Pz IV of 12. Panzer-Division knocked out by the artillery of the Leningrad Front, February 1944. (Georgy Lukin collection)

Soviet infantry and BA-10M armored cars attack a village during the Leningrad – Novgorod Operation, January 1944. (RinP)

The Leningrad–Novgorod motorway, January 1944. A column of soldiers of the Volkhov Front passing the wreck of a German staff car and the bodies of dead German troops. (RinP)

THE NOVGOROD OFFENSIVE

The Volkhov Front went over to the offensive on 14 January, i.e. simultaneously with the right wing of the Leningrad Front attacking from the Oranienbaum Bridgehead. As planned, the main blow was delivered by 59th Army of Lieutenant-General Korovnikov. Its mission was the destruction of the German force defending Novgorod, liberation of the town and securing the Leningrad–Moscow railroad.

The army was to strike with two 'shock' groups, deployed on the flanks, which had to mount pincer attacks, thereby completely encircling Novgorod. The stronger of the two was assembled some 30 km to the north of the place, on the left bank of the Volkhov. It consisted not only of rifle divisions and artillery, but also nearly all the tanks placed at the disposal of Korovnikov. The other one was gathered in the vicinity of Lake Ilmen, just south of Novgorod. Subsequently, upon taking the town, the army was to advance to the west/southwest, capture Luga and cut off the retreat routes of the Germans to Pskov. In the meantime, the 8th and 54th Armies, which were positioned further north, were to attack toward Tosno and Lyuban. By doing so, they had to pin down the opposing enemy forces and prevent them from being transferred to the endangered Novgorod area.

The three armies of Meretskov's Volkhov Front were opposed by the weaker part of Lindemann's 18. Army: three corps (XXVI., XXVIII. and XXXVIII. Army Corps) with just seven divisions (three of which unreliable Luftwaffe field divisions), a battle group of the 4. SS-Polizei-Panzergrenadier-Division and a Latvian Waffen-SS brigade. There were also several independent infantry regiments and battalions, heavy artillery units, combat engineers, three anti-tank companies and even a bizarre unit called the 'Spanish Blue Legion', which was supposed to be the ancestor of the Blue Division, but in reality was a demoralized useless addition to the order of battle of the 121. Infanterie-Division.

During the twenty eight months of predominately static warfare the Germans had constructed two major defensive belts: one between Novgorod and Chudovo, and one along the right bank of the Kerest River (a branch of the Volkhov). Furthermore, they had transformed a number of settlements situated in their rear into strongholds, including the towns of Novgorod, Chudovo, Lyuban, Tosno, Mga and Luga. Novgorod, for instance, was especially heavy fortified: it was surrounded by three defensive lines, while all solid buildings in the town itself were converted into bunkers. Hopes were high that these measures would slow down the Soviet advance and allow the Germans to conduct an orderly withdrawal.

Pz.Kpfw. V 'Panther' Ausf. D of I./Panzer-Regiment 29 knocked-out by the Soviet artillery and abandoned on the road to Kingisepp, January 1944. (TsAMO)

* * *

Contrary to the expectations of the Soviet generals, during the first day of the offensive (14 January) Korovnikov's 59th Army gained very little ground. The well-entrenched Germans fought back with great vigor, let alone that the heavy snowfall grounded the Red Air Force and obscured the visibility of artillery targets. Worse still, the tanks bogged down in the swamps. Not surprisingly, by the evening the assault detachments of the northern 'shock' group had advanced no more than 600–1,000 meters. An especially important role in the containment of the Soviet onslaught was played by the inexperienced soldiers of 1. Luftwaffen-Feld-Division and the always dreadful 8.8 cm heavy flak batteries used in a ground-combat role.

The southern 'shock' group, which was led by Major-General Svilkin, was more successful. During the night preceding the offensive some Soviet infantry units crossed Ilmen Lake over the frozen surface and in so doing outflanked the German

Sd.Kfz. 250 light armored halftrack knocked-out in the vicinity of Gostilitsy, at the edge of the Oranienbaum Bridgehead, January 1944. (TsAMO)

German gun destroyed by Soviet artillery, January 1944. (TsAMO)

German 10.5 cm leFH 18 light howitzer destroyed by the artillery of 2nd Shock Army, January 1944. (TsAMO)

German 2 cm Flak silenced by artillery of 2nd Shock Army, January 1944. (TsAMO)

German vehicles and equipment destroyed by artillery of 2nd Shock Army, January 1944. (TsAMO)

main line of resistance to the south. Having infiltrated into the immediate rear of the enemy, Svilkin's spearheads managed to capture several villages during the light part of the day.

Generaloberst Lindemann was well aware that in its present state the Novgorod sector would not last long and so rushed part of his tiny tactical reserves to the area, namely Oberst Appelt's Grenadier-Regiment 102 (of the 24. Infanterie-Division) and a cavalry detachment, as well as elements of some field-replacement battalions, a Latvian and an Estonian auxiliary battalions, and even an ad-hoc unit made of soldiers on leave. However, it was apparent that the command of the 18. Army was scraping the bottom of the barrel and the collapse of the German front at Novgorod was just a matter of time.

Korovnikov was by no means satisfied by the way things had developed and so decided to increase the pressure on the enemy by committing the second echelons of both 'shock' groups. The battles intensified on 15-16 January in the entire area north of Lake Ilmen. Finally, by the end of Day 3 the German defense was penetrated and the Soviets severed the Novgorod–Chudovo railway.

During the following days the progress of the 59th Army continued to be very slow. Nevertheless, its troops kept tightening the noose around Novgorod. Thus, on 18 January the southern 'shock' group of General Svilkin cut off the railroad between Novgorod and Shimsk. Two days later the northern 'shock' group reached the Novgorod–Batetsky railroad. The main reason for the slow advance of the Soviets, beyond doubt, was the stiff German resistance. But there were also other factors that contributed to the poor progress of Korovnikov's army: lack of roads, soft terrain and dense forests. All this didn't allow the two 'shock' groups to complete the encirclement of the German troops holding Novgorod on time. As a consequence, the latter were still able to maneuver their tactical reserves.

In a desperate attempt to save the front at Novgorod from crumbling, Feldmarschall von Küchler sent troops from neighboring sectors, namely the 8. Jäger-Division and the 21. and 121. Infanterie-Divisions. But the situation was already beyond repair. The only way to spare the XXXVIII. Army Corps was to immediately pull it out of the trap and this was exactly what General Lindemann did.

The respective order was issued on the night of 19/20 January. The breakout began without delay. Protected by the darkness, the Germans surged forward armed only with firearms. Often they were forced to clear their way in bitter hand-to-hand fighting, in which bayonets and hand grenades were extensively used. The clever leadership, strict discipline and exceptional leadership displayed by the jaegers and grenadiers

15 cm Panzerwerfer 42 Sd.Kfz.4/1 self-propelled rocket launcher captured by 2nd Shock Army, January 1944. The vehicle most probably belonged to 23. (Panzer) Batterie of schweres Werfer-Regiment 3. (TsAMO)

15 cm Panzerwerfer 42 Sd.Kfz. 4/1 self-propelled rocket launcher captured by 2nd Shock Army, January 1944. The vehicle most probably belonged to 23. (Panzer) Batterie of schweres Werfer-Regiment 3. (TsAMO)

allowed them eventually to reach friendly lines. It was a success, but the cost they had paid in terms of human life and materiel was huge: the escapees had to leave behind not only their towed weapons and equipment, but also nearly all heavily wounded comrades. The chief medical officer of the Silesian 28. Jäger-Division and a certain Oberfeldwebel Maurer volunteered to stay with the latter, hoping that the Russians would show mercy and would spare them.

Even though the bulk of the XXXVIII. Army Corps managed to break out, not all of the encircled troops were that lucky. Several resolute counterattacks were launched but many of the splinter groups were destroyed by Korovnikov's men in the forests west of Novgorod. About 3,000 of them were taken prisoner.

The Soviets entered the deserted and ruined Novgorod on the morning of 20 January. By then the escapees, who were nothing more than a motley crowd of battle-weary soldiers, were already setting up a new defensive line some 20 km west of the town. It was a clever move on the part of the German command that was well-executed by Oberst Appelt, the commander of Grenadier-Regiment 102, and his men. The frontline in that sector was stabilized for a while and the advance of the 59th Army checked. Not surprisingly, in the first days of February 1944, Appelt and his three battalion commanders were each awarded the Knight's Cross for their role in the successful breakout from the Novgorod cauldron.

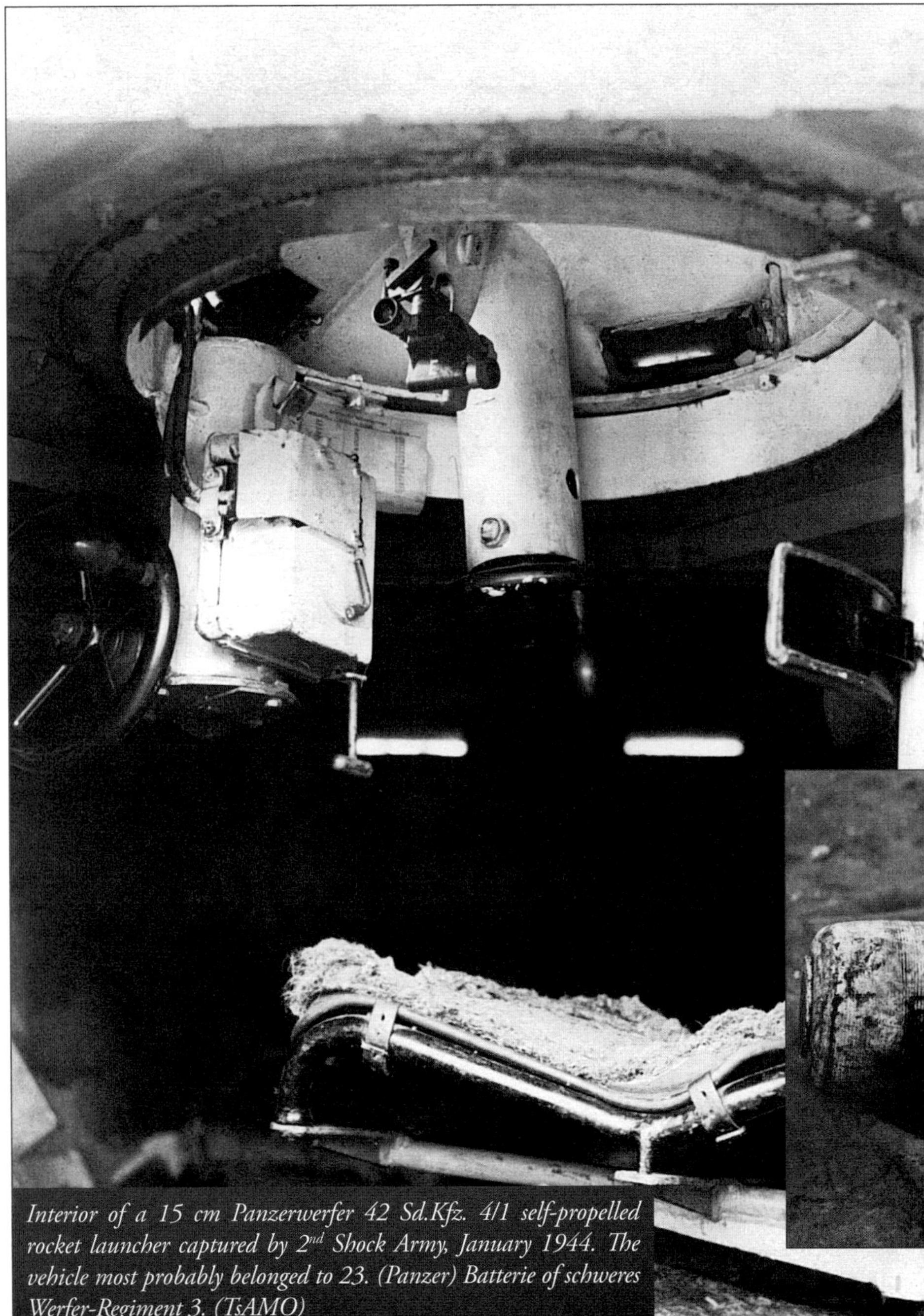

Interior of a 15 cm Panzerwerfer 42 Sd.Kfz. 4/1 self-propelled rocket launcher captured by 2nd Shock Army, January 1944. The vehicle most probably belonged to 23. (Panzer) Batterie of schweres Werfer-Regiment 3. (TsAMO)

Wgr. 41 projectile for 15 cm Panzerwerfer captured by 2nd Shock Army, January 1944. (TsAMO)

Various types of artillery pieces abandoned by the Germans during their retreat from the area of the Oranienbaum Bridgehead, January 1944. (TsAMO)

German 10.5 cm leFH 18 light howitzer destroyed by artillery of 2nd Shock Army, January 1944. (TsAMO)

StuG III Ausf F L/43 assault gun knocked out by 2nd Shock Army, January 1944. (TsAMO)

* * *

The other two armies of the Volkhov Front also contributed to the Soviet victory at Novgorod by engaging the enemy forces facing them. The 54th Army of Lieutenant-General Roginsky, for instance, went over to the offensive on 16 January and immediately pinned down the opposing XXVI. and XXVIII. Army Corps. The battle lasted five more days, during which the army gained about 5 km of ground.

Pressed from above, General Lindemann ordered the vicinity of Chudovo and Lyuban to be held at any cost. The reason behind that decision is easy to explain: the main German supply communications ran through the area in question, namely the Leningrad–Moscow railroad and motorway. Along the latter the defenders had built an important switch position, which was called the Rollbahn-Stellung. However, the Soviet success at Novgorod changed these plans very quickly. On 21 January, the 8th Army of the Volkhov

Pz.Kpfw. V 'Panther' Ausf. D tanks of I./Panzer-Regiment 29 knocked-out by artillery of 2nd Shock Army, January 1944. (TsAMO)

Sd.Kfz. 10/4 halftrack and its crew destroyed by the artillery of 2nd Shock Army. (TsAMO)

A knocked-out Pz.Kpfw. V 'Panther' Ausf. D tanks of I./Panzer-Regiment 29 abandoned on the battlefield, January 1944. (TsAMO)

Pz.Kpfw. V 'Panther' Ausf. D tanks of I./Panzer-Regiment 29 knocked-out by artillery of 2nd Shock Army, January 1944. (TsAMO)

7.5 cm Pak 40 anti-tank gun captured by 311th Rifle Regiment in the vicinity of Stary Bor, at the southern perimeter of the Oranienbaum Bridgehead, January 1944. (TsAMO)

7.5 cm Pak 40 anti-tank gun knocked out by artillery of 2nd Shock Army during the breakout from the Oranienbaum Bridgehead, 17 January 1944. (TsAMO)

Sd.Kfz. 10/4 halftrack captured on the battlefield by 2nd Shock Army, January 1944. (TsAMO)

Front captured Mga and thus threatened the entire right wing of the German 18. Army with encirclement. Now Lindemann had no other choice left but to pull his troops out of the trap as quickly as possible.

The hurried German withdrawal to the Rollbahn-Stellung forced the Soviet senior commanders to correct their plans, too. The 67th Army (of the Leningrad Front) and the Volkhov Front received orders to clear the Leningrad–Moscow railroad and Krasnogvardeysk. Subsequently, the 59th Army was to take Luga, while the 8th and 54th Armies were to take Tosno and Lyuban, respectively. The mission of the 54th Army was considered to be of primary importance and so it received reinforcements from the 67th and 8th Armies, as well as from the reserves of Volkhov Front.

Two 'Panthers' of I. /Panzer-Regiment 29 lost during the retreat of III. SS-Panzer-Corps from Oranienbaum to Narva, January 1944. (author's collection)

German military cemetery in Ropsha, halfway between the Oranienbaum Bridgehead and Leningrad, January 1944. (TsAMO)

7.5 cm Pak 40 anti-tank gun knocked out by artillery of 2nd Shock Army, January 1944. (TsAMO)

The fighting continued to be very heavy and the Germans fought vigorously for every meter of ground. Tosno was taken only on 26 January, Lyuban fell into Soviet hands two days later and Chudovo fell on 29 January. Thus, by the end of the month Meretskov's forces fully secured the Leningrad–Moscow railroad and the Rollbahn-Stellung. However, they failed to annihilate the German forces opposing them.

By the end of January 1944 the armies of the Volkhov Front had advanced between 60 and 100 km to the west. But the Germans had managed to strengthen their forces and stabilize the frontline once they occupied the 'Panther' Line. Especially important was the role played by the 12. Panzer-Division, which had been quickly transferred from the Vitebsk area in northeastern Byelorussia. Therefore, it was not surprising that by 1 February Meretskov's offensive had begun to lose momentum.

The situation in the sector of Meretskov's northern neighbor, the Leningrad Front, was not that much different. On 31 January the forward detachments of the 2nd Shock Army crossed the Luga River and launched a resolute attack on Kingisepp. On the next day the town was completely secured. This local success was immediately exploited by Fedyuninsky and before long his troops established bridgeheads on the western bank of the Narva River. Further south the 42nd Army captured much more ground – having crossed the Luga on 27 January, on 4 February they took the town of Gdov, which was situated on the eastern shore of Lake Peipus.

* * *

The three armies of Meretskov's Volkhov Front were not able to catch up with the pace of the Leningrad Front. Their main mission was still the same: to capture Luga. The 59th and 8th Armies advanced on the town from the east, while the 54th Army advanced from the northeast. But their advance was very slow owing the stiff German resistance. Being well aware of the importance of Luga as a junction and a stronghold, the new commander of Army Group 'North' Generaloberst Model (von Küchler was sacked by Hitler on 31 January) assembled there all the forces he could grab at that moment. Given the above, it was not a surprise that Luga fell into Soviet hands only on 12 February.

Stalin was very disappointed by the performance of Meretskov and his staff and, on 15 February 1944, ordered the Volkhov Front to be disbanded. The 8th, 54th and 59th Armies were placed under the neighboring Leningrad Front of General Govorov, while the 1st Shock Army (it fought briefly under Meretskov during the first half of February) was returned back to the 2nd Baltic Front.

Thus ended Operation 'January Thunder'. By 15 February both the Volkhov and Leningrad Fronts had liberated 779 settlements and towns. They had advanced between 50 and 120 km to the west thereby completely removing any threat to Leningrad. Of particular importance was the clearing of the railroad and motorway to Moscow, which improved the logistical capabilities of both fronts and also the supply situation of the civilian population.

However, a new problem had already emerged. Since Meretskov had clearly failed to capture Luga in accordance with the time-tables, the Soviet High Command found itself forced to redirect troops of the Leningrad Front (namely from the 42nd and 67th Armies) to the south. As result of this, the pressure of the Red Army on the critical Narva sector decreased and the Germans were able to bring to a halt the Soviet offensive in one of the most sensitive points of the Eastern Front. Thus, the stage was set for yet another epic battle – that of Narva.

CHAPTER 3

THE RAID OF THE 16TH TANK BRIGADE

During the battle for Novgorod the 16th Tank Brigade of Colonel Urvanov was employed as a forward detachment of the 6th Rifle Corps. (It was part of the northern 'shock' group of the 59th Army). The brigade comprised of two tank battalions totaling 48 machines (32 T-34/76,9 T-70 and 7 T-60) and a battalion of tank-riding submachine gunners.

The mission of the brigade was, by sneaking through the gap in the German main line of resistance between the villages of Koptsy and Tyutitnsy, to attack to the southwest and by the end of Day 3 to capture Vyazhische. Subsequently, the brigade was to cut off the German supply lines in the general direction of the Lyubolyady train station.

The gap in the German defenses (between Koptsy and Tyutitnsy) was to be torn open by the infantry of the 239th Rifle Division and the tanks of the 35th Independent Tank Regiment. Only then would Urvanov's brigade be unleashed and break into open country.

* * *

The Soviet offensive began at 10:50 MT (Moscow Time) on 14 January 1944 and right from the outset encountered very stiff resistance put up by the Silesian 28. Jäger-Division. Even though the Red infantry succeeded in breaching the first two defensive belts (full-depth trenches reinforced with wooden beams), they paid dearly for that success: the murderous German fire had put out of action nearly all of the tanks of the 35th Regiment. Worse still, the third German defensive belt was still intact. It looked formidable: a full-depth trench line on the western bank of the Pitba River shielded by an embankment reinforced with wooden beams; the approaches to the latter were protected by a 300- m-wide minefield. This left the command of the 59th Army no other choice but to prematurely commit to battle the 16th Tank Brigade and use it as a through assault formation instead of an exploitation force.

The attack by the 239th Rifle Division resumed during the night of 15/16 January 1944. It was preceded by the usual very intense artillery bombardment. Before long, the close-support and bomber units of the 14th Air Army also joined the softening-up operation. Special attention was paid to the sector where the tank brigade would be committed. There the 'Shturmoviks' and bombers reportedly destroyed 9 Nebelwerfers, two 15 cm artillery batteries, two anti tank batteries and a Flak battery. During the third pass over the positions of the Silesian division the Soviet pilots focused their efforts on the German field fortifications. This allowed them to also demolish the main trench line and several earth bunkers, thereby denying the badly battered Jaegers shelter and protection. It should be mentioned here that 'Stalin's falcons' wouldn't have been so successful without the guidance of Major Kirilenko, a forward radio controller of the 14th Air Army who had been placed in a tank with a long-range radio.

The softening-up apparently worked because the initial push of the brigade brought quick success: the third German defensive belt was breached, the embankment was overcome and the tanks reached the western bank of the Pitba. Their further advance, however, was checked by the complete absence of roads as well as by the above-mentioned minefield. The latter was not detected early enough and the first three tanks that went over it detonated. These sudden losses called for an immediate intervention of mine-clearing squads. The brigade's sappers, as well as those provided by 239th Rifle Division, immediately stepped forward and began to remove the lethal explosives. They managed to complete their dangerous job and open passages for the tanks despite murderous enemy fire.

It seemed now that nothing could stop the brigade from going forward but the soft ground and the lack of river crossings once again hindered the forward movement of the heavy tanks and artillery pieces. Wasting no time, the men began to build bridges. Every kind of wooden material they could lay their hands upon – planks, logs, timber – was put into use. Nevertheless, the bridge-building process proceeded slowly since there was nothing else in the vicinity. It was only at 1:00-1:30 MT that the crossing was completed and the brigade moved to the western bank of the Pitba.

* * *

During the battles to the west of the river the brigade was assembled as follows: it was spearheaded by a reconnaissance group of 3 T-34 tanks with 12-14 infantrymen riding on each of them. It was the first to cross the Pitba and reach the northern limits of Tyutsy. Together with the tanks (and often ahead of them) an officer-led engineering squad operated.

The main body of the brigade followed in the wake of the reconnaissance group. It rolled forward in a two-column formation (1st Battalion on the right and 2nd Battalion on the left), advancing on a frontage of up to 300 m each. There were about 15-17 T-34 tanks in each of the battalions. The lighter tanks (the T-60s and the T-70s) followed behind them. The entire battalion of submachine gunners (up to 250 men) rode on the tanks.

The 511th Rifle Regiment of the 239th Rifle Division followed behind the brigade. It is noteworthy that neither then, nor during ensuing raid in the German rear zone, was the infantry able to catch up with the tanks. That's why after 19 January, when the brigade finally broke into open country, it operated as a fully independent force, way ahead of the nearest friendly infantry formation.

All elements of the brigade communicated with each other by radio. Colonel Urvanov could communicate with his tanks, artillery, infantry and air force. His command tank was constantly with the combat units, usually immediately behind the 2nd Battalion.

Colonel Kirill Urvanov, commander of 16th Tank Brigade. (Leonid Gorchakov)

Apart from its organic units, the brigade was additionally reinforced by the 1433rd Self-Propelled Artillery Regiment of Lieutenant-Colonel Morev which had just five SU-85 guns. The terrain, however, was broken and marshy, and the self-propelled guns were not able to catch up with the tanks. (Usually they got stuck in morasses.) Only one gun managed to overcome the unfavorable ground to render support to the 2nd Battalion. During the later stages of the battle, when the brigade attacked along the motorway in the direction of Shimsk, the regiment was able to prove its worth. Then its machines gave invaluable support to Urvanov's troops.

* * *

Upon crossing the Pitba, the tanks outflanked Tyutsy to the north and then turned to the west, then to the southwest, along the route of the railway and a little to the east of it. No minefields were encountered and the pace of the unit's advance accelerated. Not surprisingly, the brigade was then in a more advantageous position than the Germans, since the latter had no prepared positions in their rear and were forced to roll back their main battle line.

From 14 to 16 January 1944 the units of 16th Tank Brigade secured the Podberezie train station, inflicting heavy losses on the German 28. Jäger-Division in the process. A considerable amount of booty was captured, including wagonloads of ammunition and vehicles. (TsAMO)

The Soviet tanks advanced on Podberezie and, by 09:00 MT on 16 January, captured the train station of the same name. Shortly before that, a small detachment had swiftly secured the railroad booth at the intersection of the motorway and the railway.

The new situation (the raid in the unprotected enemy rear) forced Urvanov to make changes in the order of battle of the brigade. The reconnaissance group was still in the lead, followed by the 1st and 2nd Battalions that now rolled forward in a column formation, one after the other, separated by a distance of 1-2 km. They encountered strong fire from Tyutsy, the forest west of Andryukhinovo and from Podberezie. This forced the tankers to call in the artillery. The friendly infantry did the same.

As mentioned above, the Podberezie train station was captured at 09:00 MT by the reconnaissance group. It encountered relatively light resistance. The tank battalions arrived at the station around 11:00-12:00 MT.

The rifle division was still not maintaining permanent contact with the brigade. While the tanks were outflanking Tyutsy to the west and north, the infantrymen struck the village from the east. Upon clearing the place, they attacked Andryukhinovo. Part of the division was also involved in mopping-up small German splinter groups sneaking through the area.

The other Soviet armored formation operating in that sector – the 29th Independent Tank Brigade – also performed well. It cooperated successfully with Urvanov's men and upon breaking into open country advanced on the village of Nekokhovo. By 21:30 MT on 16 January, the reconnaissance group of the 29th Tank Brigade reached Nekokhovo–Podberezie road at Hill 39, thereby cutting off this important enemy communication artery. Now all German retreat routes were effectively blocked. This would bring grave consequences for some of the Wehrmacht units engaged in that area.

* * *

At 21:30 MT on 16 January, a long column of Panzerjäger-Abteilung 28 (the anti-tank unit of 28. Jäger-Division) was spotted moving along the road from Podberezie to the west, towards Nekokhovo. It comprised 45 vehicles, 15 motorcycles and 12 Pak 40 heavy AT guns. The Germans failed to spot the Soviet ambush at the Podberezie station and almost reached Hill 39, where the reconnaissance group of the 29th Independent Tank Brigade was waiting. At that moment the 16th Brigade struck the rear end of the column while the reconnaissance group of the 29th Brigade attacked its head. The Germans were caught off guard and completely decimated. Up to 400 dead bodies remained on the snow-covered battlefield.

By the morning of 17 January the reconnaissance group of the 16th Tank Brigade, together with the brigade's main body, rolled to the southwest, in the general direction of Vyazhische and the Bolotnaya station on orders from above. By 19:00 MT the reconnaissance group reached the Bolotnaya station where a small German garrison was quickly annihilated. The success was immediately radioed to Colonel Urvanov. Shortly afterwards the rest of the brigade arrived at the station, too. During the day it had encountered no resistance at all.

It is worth mentioning that the brigade was still operating on its own. The 239th Rifle Division was lagging some 3-4 km behind. There was no artillery support, either – the artillery was with the infantry, the self-propelled regiment was struggling with the terrain and only one of its SU guns could take part in the action.

The role played by the sappers in combat is usually underestimated, but during those days of intense mobile warfare they fully proved their worth. A detachment of the brigade's combat engineers were assigned to the reconnaissance group, while the rest accompanied the main body of the brigade, but both parties performed very well. One has to take into account that the terrain conditions were quite difficult; there were many rivers and streams that had to be forded, and in order not to lose the momentum of the offensive, the brigade had to build bridges/crossings from every kind of material its men could lay their hands on. Colonel Urvanov's approach to the situation was very flexible – he repeatedly shifted the engineers between the reconnaissance group and the bulk of the brigade, depending on where they were needed most.

7.5 cm Pak 40 anti-tank gun and its RSO tractor knocked out by tanks of 16th Tank Brigade during the taking of the Podberezie train station. (TsAMO)

* * *

Upon assembling at the Bolotnaya station, Colonel Urvanov received orders to take Vyazhische. He decided to capture the place by pincer attacks – his 16th Tank Brigade was to outflank the village to the northwest, while the arriving 29th Tank Brigade, which was now placed under him, was to attack from the southeast. However, before long it turned out that the 29th had stuck on the road and was unable to take part in the action. Thus, once again the men of the 16th could only rely on themselves.

The assault commenced on the same evening. Having moved through the Bolotnaya station, at about 22:30 MT on 17 January the reconnaissance group and the 1st Battalion were in contact with the enemy at the northeastern limits of Vyazhische. In the meantime the submachine gunners dismounted at the barn northwest of the village. They approached their objective on foot and reached the northeastern limits of Vyazhische unnoticed, without firing a single shot. In the meantime the tanks that were already fighting at the northwestern outskirts of the village succeeded in diverting the attention of the German mortar crews. In so doing they hoped to assist the submachine gunners in breaking into the settlement by surprise. Then, however, the tankers made a mistake: they fired several flares that erroneously illuminated the dismounted friendly tank riders. The Germans immediately redirected their fire, the Soviet submachine gunners sustained losses and were forced to take cover.

The performance of the brigade during that action was largely unsatisfactory. The reconnaissance group had failed to gather any intelligence and the tankers were forced to approach their objective very cautiously, since they had no idea of the strength of the German garrison in front of them or exactly where the Germans had set up their field fortifications. Vyazhische was captured only by 01:00 MT on 18 January. The infantry of the 239th Rifle Division arrived within the next two hours and spent the rest of night mopping up the remaining enemy pockets of resistance in the village.

Until the morning of 19 January the brigade was not involved in combat. It was badly needed on the battlefield since the encirclement of the German forces defending Novgorod was far from complete but it had to stay behind due to a serious shortage of ammunition. The road to Vyazhische was still not fully cleared and other roads leading to the battlefield were jammed by traffic so the trucks carrying shells simply could not get through. Apart from that, many tanks were in need of repair.

In an attempt to deal with the critical situation transport planes were requested from the 14th Air Army. They were ready to take off but finally, on the morning of 19 January, the trucks arrived, the tanks' ammunition was replenished and the brigade was again combat-worthy. Thus Colonel Urvanov and his aides learned an important lesson regarding the correct planning of supplies and logistics.

* * *

On 19 January the brigade was ordered to continue its advance in the general direction of the Naschi siding and a meat-packing plant. In the morning the reconnaissance group comprising 3-4 tanks with mounted submachine gunners and sappers set out for the Naschi siding. Their jump-off point was the monastery in Vyazhische. The tanks moved through the forest, where there were no roads at all. The tankers were supported by the infantrymen of the 511th Rifle Regiment (239th Rifle Division). From that moment on the latter never separated from the T-34s. Moreover, sometimes they even advanced ahead of them.

By 15:00 MT the tanks and the infantry reached the railroad and blocked it. Shortly afterwards the main body of the brigade arrived, too, and took over the blocking position while the reconnaissance group and the 511th Regiment resumed their advance toward the meat-packing plant.

Vehicle column belonging to a German anti-tank battalion (Panzerjäger-Abteilung 28 of 28. Jäger-Division) destroyed during the fighting at Podberezie. (TsAMO)

Column of vehicles belonging to German anti-tank battalion (Panzerjäger-Abteilung 28 of 28. Jäger-Division) destroyed during the fighting at Podberezie. (TsAMO)

German equipment destroyed by 16th Tank Brigade during the battle for Novgorod. (Leonid Gorchakov)

German positions and equipment destroyed by 16th Tank Brigade during the battle for Novgorod. (Leonid Gorchakov)

Field repair of damaged T-34 of 16th Tank Brigade. (TsAMO)

The raid of the Soviet tanks once again escaped the notice of the German command. Much to the surprise of the defenders of Novgorod, their attempts to retreat along the railroad and the motorway were checked by the reconnaissance group and the 511th Regiment, which by then already had secured the meat-packing plant. These splinter groups were usually hunted down and destroyed by the Soviet tanks and infantrymen.

The Germans found themselves in a hopeless situation. Having realized there was no way out of the Novgorod cauldron, they intensified their breakout attempts. On the evening of 19 January the tankers and the submachine-gun battalion of the 16th Tank Brigade alone had repelled 11 enemy counterattacks launched in the westerly direction. These counterattacks were largely unsuccessful. The battlefield was covered with the bodies of more than 750 dead German soldiers. The tactics used by the Soviet submachine gunners proved especially effective. Having occupied suitable defensive positions, they allowed the Germans to come close and opened up with devastating fire from all their weapons from a distance of just 30-40 meters. The

Camouflage painting and evacuation of damaged KV-1 from the battlefield. (TsAMO)

Tank crews of 16th Tank Brigade who had distinguished themselves during the battle for Novgorod. (Leonid Gorchakov)

Tank crews of 16th Tank Brigade who had distinguished themselves during the battle for Novgorod. (Leonid Gorchakov)

commander of the submachine-gun battalion, Captain Sosunov, showed a great deal of composure and, not surprisingly, during those clashes his men inflicted terrible losses on the desperate Germans. The tanks of the brigade could not operate on the marshy ground and so remained on the road to be employed as fixed firing points.

The 511th Regiment also played an important role in decimating the escaping German garrison of Novgorod. On that day the riflemen blocked the road leading from the town to the west and inflicted heavy losses on the escapees.

The actions of the 16th Independent Tank Brigade from 16 to 20 January were considered to be a success. Moving over very difficult terrain, in a matter of four days it had covered 34 kilometers (i.e. roughly 8.5 km a day). The brigade's reconnaissance group in particular distinguished itself and maintained constant contact with Colonel Urvanov by radio.

* * *

The leadership of the 59th Army was very satisfied by the performance of the brigade during the Novgorod Operation. After the battle, some conclusions were drawn concerning the employment of armored units in fast-changing situations. By 31 January 1944 they were summarized by Lieutenant-Colonel Ivanov, the head of army's combat-experience department, as follows:

The operation proved that mobile detachments made of tank units reinforced with infantry play a very important role in wrecking havoc in the enemy rear. Tanks with mounted infantry could operate independently.

The cooperation of the armored units with the air force is maintained when a forward air controller is placed in a tank with a powerful two-way radio.

The tanks could operate outside the main road network when reinforced with sappers outfitted with a sufficient amount of engineering equipment. This allowed them to overcome difficult terrain, including forests and swamps. Especially important proved to be the decision to assign engineers to the reconnaissance group.

The assigned self-propelled artillery must be used only when the terrain conditions allow since the cross-country capabilities of the SU guns were inferior to that of the tanks.

When two tank formations use the same road, there is sometimes a slowing down of the advance. Instead, they must move on/along parallel roads. This would allow them to commit their units much faster, achieve boldness and surprise.

It is very important to maintain the pace of advance in mobile warfare. That's why it is very important to constantly supply the fighting tank units with fuel and ammunition. Any breakdown in the supply system will lead to halting the advance of the tanks. This can be prevented only if the supply bases and workshops are repeatedly moved forward by prime movers and cross-country trucks.

CHAPTER 4

THE FIRST BATTLE OF NARVA, FEBRUARY – APRIL 1944

THE NARVA POSITION: STRATEGIC AND POLITICAL IMPORTANCE

Once the Red Army reached the prewar Estonian border, Stalin ordered the attacks to continue without operational pause. Like every other warlord, he was afraid of losing the momentum of the entire offensive. The new assignment of the Leningrad Front was to destroy the enemy forces holding the strategically important Narva Isthmus and push deep into Estonia. Stalin's main strategic goal was pretty clear: rapidly retaking the country, which subsequently would be turned into a supply and military base for a further expansion into the Baltic region. There was also no doubt that a Soviet victory would push Finland out of the war.

Hitler, in turn, was very determined to hold the 'Panther' Line (and in particular the Narva position). Not surprisingly, his reasons were the same as Stalin's, i.e. they were political as well military in nature. The Fuehrer's biggest fear was that Finland, his northernmost ally, would seek peace with the Soviet Union. This would force the Finns to quit their support for the Waffen SS and Wehrmacht mountain troops fighting on the arctic front. Worse still, then the Third Reich would also be evicted from the Petsamo area, whose precious nickel mines were of great importance for the production of arms and munitions.

THE ORGANIZATION OF ARMEEABTEILUNG 'NARWA'

By 26 January 1944 the German 18. Army was effectively split in two. There was a 20 km gap between its northern flank, which was retreating westwards toward Kingisepp and Narva, and the bulk of the army which was falling back to the southwest, in the direction of Luga and Pskov.

The northern group combined the III. SS-Panzer-Corps and the LIV. Army Corps of General der Infanterie Otto Sponheimer. The latter was put in charge of both corps and thus a new task force, designated Gruppe 'Sponheimer', came into being.

Gruppe 'Sponheimer' successfully retreated behind the Narva River, even though this was done in very heavy and bloody fighting. Wasting no time, the badly mauled divisions began to occupy the 'Panther' Line.

By the end of January 1944 the gap between Sponheimer's two corps and rest of the army had grown to about 50 km. The Soviets were enjoying complete freedom of movement and were threatening to overrun the 'Panther' Line. The situation had become extremely precarious. The condition of the troops of Gruppe 'Sponheimer' required controls close to the front, but the HQ of the 18. Army, which had its hands full southeast of Lake Peipus, was no longer able to provide that. The physical separation of the combat formations, as well as the lack of signal communications, required a new solution to be found. Accordingly, shortly after midnight of 3/4 February, Gruppe 'Sponheimer' was assigned directly to the Army Group 'North'.

It was apparent that Gruppe 'Sponheimer' was nothing more than a temporary measure. That's why, at the request of General Model, a new army headquarters was organized and given control of the Narva sector. The staff of the former LIV. Army Corps became the nucleus of the new army staff. Elements were ceded also from the command staffs of both Army Group 'North' and the 18. Army, and in so doing the new Sponheimer's staff was brought up to the minimum strength necessary for the operation of an army. Coordination with the air force and the navy was ensured by strong liaison detachments provided by Luftwaffe and Kriegsmarine, respectively.

In February 1944 the new formation was given the official designation Armeeabteilung 'Narwa' (Army Detachment 'Narva'). It also got a new commander - General der Infanterie Johannes Friessner, a Knight's Cross holder, who until recently was in charge of the XXIII. Army Corps.

Thus formed, the new Armeeabteilung took over the sector of the 'Panther' Line from the northwestern edge of Lake Peipus to the Baltic coast, as well as the coastal defenses as far as Tallinn. 290 of 330 km of this defensive line were fronted by water.

Given the high strategic importance assigned to the Narva area, the Armeeabteilung was rapidly beefed up. In March it already numbered ten divisions, one brigade and several combat-support units divided between three corps staffs. Some of these divisions were transferred from remote areas such as Byelorussia and Norway, the rest were redeployed from neighboring sectors within Army Group 'North'. Its total ration strength (as per 1 March 1944) was 123,541 men, which demolishes the myth of the multi-fold Soviet numerical superiority on the Narva front.

Model was well aware of the importance of the Narva position and so deployed some of his best formations there. The only exception was perhaps the inexperienced 214. Infanterie-Division that had arrived from Norway as a last-ditch reserve. Like most of the so-called 'occupational' divisions, it was very weak organizationally – just four infantry battalions and two light artillery battalions. Not surprisingly, it quickly lost its combat worth and by the second half of March 1944 it was pulled out of the front for reconstitution.

Another interesting formation was the Estonian 20. SS-Grenadier-Division that just had been formed from recruits and volunteers, plus a small German core personnel. Apparently, it was committed to battle quite unfinished, because in February it numbered about 6,000 men. The Estonian division fought well during the opening phase of the battle but during the summer campaign was de facto disbanded and its elements distributed among the neighboring German formations.

Waffen-SS troops change positions somewhere between Leningrad and Narva. (author's collection)

NARVA OR PSKOV?

The first battle of Narva was a direct continuation of the Soviet Operation 'January Thunder' that had driven the German invaders back from the gates of Leningrad. On 1 February, the very day when his forces took Kingisepp, General Govorov submitted a report to Stalin outlining the scope of his next offensive move: the 'liberation of Estonia and taking the entire southern coast of the Gulf of Finland'. In order to achieve this, the Leningrad Front had to reach the Luga and the Narva rivers along their entire length, and, wasting no time, secure bridgeheads on the western bank of the latter. Then the German position at Narva had to be crushed, thereby opening the way to the Estonian capital. In order to achieve this, Govorov proposed that the weight of the Soviet attacks should be shifted from Pskov to Narva, i.e. from the Volkhov Front to the right wing of the Leningrad Front (his reasoning was that Narva offered the shortest route to Estonia's heartland). The Kremlin dictator agreed with him and shortly afterwards the Volkhov Front was dissolved.

Subsequent events proved Govorov right. On 2/3 February the 2nd Shock Army was already at the Narva, capturing bridgeheads at several places on its western bank. On 4 February, the 42nd Army took the town of Gdov, a major stronghold on the eastern shore of Lake Peipus. The German force defending the Gdov area (58. Infanterie-Division) was encircled and succeeded in breaking out at the cost of heavy losses. It is estimated that the division lost about a third of its manpower and nearly all of its materiel.

On the other hand, the advance of the front's left wing, as well as that of Meretskov's Volkhov Front, was already losing its momentum. Having encountered stiff enemy resistance, the 67th Army was halted at the distant approaches to Luga. The repeated German counterattacks proved especially effective – time and again grenadiers supported by small groups of tanks/assault guns struck back at the Soviets, literally breaking down their attacks. The culmination of their efforts was the sharp counterthrust delivered by the recently arrived 12. Panzer-Division that finally closed the gap between the 16. and 18. Armies. Much to the horror of the Soviet High Command, it seemed that the battle was heading for a stalemate.

At Luga the new commander of Army Group 'North', Generaloberst Model, clearly demonstrated why he was regarded as a master of the active defense. By constantly shifting his reserves, he almost brought the advance of the Red steamroller to a halt and thus allowed the forces retreating to the southwest, towards Pskov, to do so in a relatively orderly fashion. The turning point came on 5 February when a strong German battle group (12. Panzer Division and some infantry units) launched resolute counterattacks against the Soviet forces that had penetrated along the Luga–Pskov motorway. Up to 9,000 men of the 8th Army (the bulk of two rifle divisions), plus some partisans, found themselves caught in a trap in the deep rear of the German 18. Army. Over the course of the next twelve days they were involved in a battle of life and death against overwhelming odds until they were relieved on 15 February. By then about half of them had been either killed or wounded. Shortly afterwards the officer in charge of the encircled group (Colonel Koziev, the commander of the 256th Rifle Division) was awarded the highest Soviet military award – Hero of the Soviet Union Golden Star.

Even though Luga fell on 12 February 1944, the German front didn't collapse. As result of the measures undertaken by Generaloberst Lindemann, by mid-February 1944 the entire perimeter of the 18. Army had been consolidated. All gaps, even the minor ones, had been closed by well-directed counterattacks. The army now stood in a large semi-circle whose shoulders touched Lakes Peipus and Ilmen.

The German High Command, however, was aware that in the long run this overstretched position had very little prospect of success. There were no tactical reserves left, let alone that the 18. Army was running low on troops – during the second half of January 1944 it had lost ca. 14,000 killed and 35,000 wounded, and, despite the arrival of some reinforcements, its infantry strength had dropped from 58,000 to a mere 17,000. A shortening of the frontline was necessary, especially if the Germans wanted to hold the crumbling front at Narva. Hitler didn't object to this and on the evening of 15 February the respective order arrived from OKH.

The withdrawal to the 'Panther' Line was uniformly planned with Army Group 'North'. It was to be carried out in stages and temporary defensive lines were to be reached by specified deadlines. Apart from that, the order specified the number of divisions to be employed in the various lines of resistance and indicated the march destinations for the units to be released. The document also regulated the occupation of the 'Panther' Line, which was to be completed by 1 March 1944. Surprisingly - or perhaps not so surprisingly - this was accomplished on time and was beyond doubt a miraculous achievement.

* * *

General Govorov was well aware that the gradual fighting withdrawal conducted by the Germans was winning Lindemann time and would allow his badly battered divisions to retreat in an orderly fashion. The tactics employed by Model were working very well for them – the retrograde movement was protected by rearguard detachments made of 1-2 battalions of infantry reinforced with machine guns, mortars, individual anti-tank guns, tanks or assault guns. They usually occupied switch positions in which settlements prepared for all-around defense were incorporated. Apart from that, the detachments were supported by heavy artillery firing from in depth positions. Upon the withdrawal of the main forces, the rearguards demolished all bridges and torched the settlements.

Given the above, the leadership of the Leningrad Front decided to outflank the retreating German forces by moving troops across the Lake Peipus. It was hoped that such a move would force Lindemann to divert part of his troops from Pskov and in so doing would facilitate the main Soviet assault on the town.

SU-152 of one of the units of the Volkhov Front overcomes a German defensive position, February 1944. (RinP)

The mission was assigned to the 108th Rifle Corps. The first step was to secure Piirissaar Island in the middle of the lake on 12 February. It was seized by a detachment of the 128th Rifle Division (a rifle battalion and a ski battalion) by midday. The enemy garrison (two penal companies and an Estonian security company) was quickly decimated. The Germans reacted quickly and the Luftwaffe launched a bombing raid but was not able to eliminate the dangerous intrusion.

The next step was setting up a bridgehead on the other side. On 14 February, the Soviet forward parties quickly moved over the frozen surface of the lake and secured a foothold on the western shore that was up to 12 km long and 2-3 km deep. Initially, the men of the 128th Rifle Division (one regiment and one additional battalion) succeeded in repelling all enemy counterattacks. On the next day, however, the Germans brought in reinforcements (presumably elements of the 11. Infanterie-Division and Estonian units) and, with the active help of the Luftwaffe close-support aircraft, pushed the defenders literally to the waterline. A full-blown panic began, and the rank and file retreated in disarray. The situation was so desperate that one of the battalion commanders and his deputy political officer committed suicide, fearing that the Germans would capture them alive. By the nightfall of 16 February the Soviet detachment was finished off. Only about 100 men succeeded in reaching friendly positions.

The Germans didn't stop there. On the morning of 24 February, a strong battle group (a reinforced battalion) supported by heavy artillery and bombers stormed Piirissaar Island. The Soviet garrison (a rifle battalion) fought back with vigor but was not able to withstand the pressure and abandoned its positions. Worse still, it sustained tremendous losses: 95 killed, 118 wounded and 8 missing.

Having failed to destroy the German 18. Army during the retreat of the latter from Leningrad, General Govorov then realized that the only way to capture Pskov and Ostrov was by a direct assault. From the beginning of March 1944 the armies of his left flank (42nd, 54th and 67th) launched several powerful attacks on the 'Panther' Line but they were beaten back with heavy losses. Eventually, the Soviets gave up and in mid-April the Leningrad Front switched over to the defensive.

By then Model was no longer in command of the army group. The defensive success achieved by his forces in the Baltic area earned him promotion to the rank of Feldmarschall on 30 March 1944. But in the meantime a very dangerous situation had developed in the Western Ukraine and he was immediately flown there. Model's new appointment was to command Army Group 'South', while Generaloberst Lindemann succeeded him as commander of Army Group 'North'.

THE OPENING STAGE OF THE BATTLE OF NARVA

On the morning of 1 February the forward parties of the 2nd Shock Army captured Kingisepp, the last major enemy stronghold before the former Soviet-Estonian border. There were strong indications that the Germans wouldn't be able to hold out for long. Thus, prisoners of the 'Nordland' and 'Nederland' captured on the same day revealed that only rearguards had been left on the Russian side of the river while the respective formations were in full retreat, let alone that they were running low of infantry and were in desperate need of replenishment. Another POW (of a security unit) confessed that panic had broken out in the town of Narva and that the rear services had begun evacuating major supply stores. Additionally, interrogation of locals showed that in December and January some trenches had been dug out along the riverbank but the defensive line, in general, remained largely unfinished.

The Soviet commanders were now convinced that victory was at hand and were determined not to miss such an opportunity. Wasting no time, General Govorov extended the frontage of the attack of the 2nd Shock Army to the south, as far as the Lake Peipus, by placing several rifle divisions from the neighboring 42nd Army under Fedyuninsky. This made the 2nd Shock Army super-strong. Now it consisted of twelve rifle divisions divided between four rifle corps, as well as two naval infantry brigades and a fortified region, plus the usual heavy artillery, engineer and tank units. Three of these rifle corps were approaching the Narva on a broad front while the fourth (30th Guards) was resting in the rear, in readiness to exploit the initial success of the former.

Optimistically, the Soviet battle plan called for a quick envelopment of Narva by pincer attacks on the either side of the town. Subsequently, it was to advance rapidly on Jõhvi, a junction settlement situated some 50 km to the west.

* * *

The right pincer arm consisted of the 43rd Rifle Corps (three rifle divisions and a naval infantry brigade). It was positioned along the riverbank from the mouth of the Narva in the north to the Ivangorod bridgehead in the south. The corps was under orders to secure bridgeheads on the opposite bank and subsequently to consolidate them into large ones that would be used as bases for further advance.

The forward parties of the 98th Rifle Division began crossing the river on the morning of 2 February. Two small bridgeheads were established – at Kudrukula and further to the south, at Riigi. During the following night three battalions of the 48th Naval Infantry Brigade also moved across and reached the outskirts of Narva-Jõesuu (Hungerburg), where heavy fighting ensued. However, all further attempts to reinforce the footholds failed. Contrary to initial expectations, the German defense stiffened.

The defenders (227. Infanterie-Division, which had just arrived from the south, plus a Kriegsmarine penal battalion and elements of 'Nordland') pinned down the Soviet second echelons with murderous fire from machine guns, auto-cannons and mortars. Many of the attackers were literally shot to pieces on the ice, while trying to cross the river. The Germans also severed the rear communications of the footholds by blowing up the ice along the left bank of the river. To make the matters worse for the hard-pressed Soviet advance detachments, the grenadiers frequently counterattacked, pushing them meter by meter back to the riverbank.

Not surprisingly, before long the Soviet bridgeheads began to collapse. The marines of the 48th Brigade were expelled from the outskirts of Narva-Jõesuu on the afternoon of 3 February; the Germans reported that 40 POWs had been taken and that the Russians had left about 200 dead on the battlefield. The remnants of the three marine battalions escaped to the right bank of the Narva during the night of 3/4 February. The losses sustained by them during the fighting on the other side of the river were staggering: 720 killed, wounded and missing.

Units of the 98th Rifle Division, which were engaged further south, fared no better. It turned out that the 'Panther' Line was very real and consisted of full-depth trenches, earth bunkers, machine-gun nests and barbed wire entanglements. The weak Soviet advance parties simply lacked the strength to exploit their initial success. Before long, they found themselves in a hellish trap. The battalion holding the perimeter at Kudruküla, for instance, had lost up to 60% of its strength by the end of 3 February (the German battle group operating in that area claimed 68 POWs and 359 dead bodies counted on the battlefield). Its remnants retreated across the river during the same night. The companies fighting at Riigi were also hit hard and, by the next day, were vaporized. Thus, these two tactically very important Soviet bridgeheads were lost for good by 4 February.

* * *

During the period in question the troops of the 2nd Shock Army also launched attacks on Ivangorod, a major fortress and settlement located on the right bank of the river, just opposite the town of Narva. Not surprisingly, the Germans had figured out the tactical importance of Ivangorod long before the beginning of the battle and had converted it into a fortified bridgehead. They were determined to hold it at any cost. That's why immediately after the fall of Kingisepp the bulk of Steiner's III. SS-Panzer-Corps was ordered to occupy the defensive perimeter along the eastern outskirts of the town.

The bridgehead was constructed in accordance with the latest German tactical regulations and manuals. There were full-depth trenches, earth bunkers, armored and concrete pillboxes and barbed-wire entanglements. Apart from that, all major suburban settlements at the approaches to the town (Lilienbach, Natalin, Dolgaya Niva, etc.) were converted into mini-fortresses and prepared for all-around defense.

A propaganda unit visits the reconnaissance battalion of the 'Nordland' Division. Narva front, February/March 1944. (National Archives of Norway)

The troops occupying them could count on extensive fire support provided not only by the usual machine guns, mortars and heavy artillery, but also by the very dangerous 8.8 cm heavy Flak pieces.

Furthermore, the defenders cleverly used all armored vehicles at their disposal, be they operational or not. They transformed the tanks and the assault guns into mobile strongpoints and integrated them into existing defensive positions. In so doing the German commanders succeeded in maximizing the density of the infantry's firepower in the focal points. Additionally, the damaged machines (four immobile Panthers and perhaps some other AFVs) were dug in and employed as fixed firing points. This proved to be a serious problem for the Soviets, who initially launched their attacks with very little artillery support and therefore had no adequate weapons to deal with the steel colossuses.

Not surprisingly, the initial attempts of the Red Army to crush the Narva bridgehead failed. On 2, 3 and 4 February the adjacent flanks of two Soviet corps (43rd and 109th) attempted to capture Ivangorod, literally from the march, but were beaten back with heavy losses. Everywhere the Soviet infantry was met by murderous fire from the well-entrenched Waffen SS troops. At Lilienbach (in the northeast of the bridgehead), for instance, the 48th Rifle Division encountered up to 15 armored firing points, 6 concrete firing points and 14 earth bunkers. But its units could do very little to silence them because strict limits had been introduced on the amount of shells that could be fired daily per barrel. The reason for that was simple: at that moment Fedyuninsky's army was critically short of trucks and only limited quantities of ammunition could be delivered to the frontline. The same applied to the guns – due to the lack of towing vehicles, about 80% of them had to be manhandled.

* * *

While the Soviet marines and infantrymen were fighting a battle of life and death between the seacoast and the Ivangorod bridgehead, a minor, but tactically very important success was achieved by Fedyuninsky's left pincer arm (122nd Rifle Corps). On the morning of 2 February elements of the 314th Rifle Division succeeded in capturing a small bridgehead on the northern bank of the Narva at the village of Vääska.

The German commanders were caught off guard because they believed that the marshy terrain had made that sector unsuitable for any river-crossing attempts. Tactical reserves were immediately dispatched to the endangered area and strict orders were issued to push the Russians into the river. Led by the reconnaissance battalion of the arriving Panzergrenadier-Division 'Feldherrnhalle', on 3 February alone the Germans launched fourteen counterattacks but all of them were beaten back with heavy losses. By nightfall the HQ of the Soviet division reported that up to 250 dead bodies had been counted on the battlefield, while another 200 enemy troops had been taken prisoner. Finally, the bridgehead at Vääska was firmly secured by the Soviets. During the following days they would enlarge it, thereby making it capable of accommodating more troops. The success was exploited immediately and from 5 February onwards one more rifle division began to move onto the northern bank of the Narva. Thus, the only foothold possessed by the 2nd Shock Army on the far side of the river would become a major jump-off point for all its further attacks and eventually would seal the fate of the entire Narva front.

Vääska was not the only place where the 122nd Rifle Corps intended to secure bridgeheads. On 5 and 6 February, the 11th and 43rd Rifle Divisions attempted to cross the river on a broad front, from Krivasoo to Permisküla, but only at one place, at Permisküla, did a single company manage to reach the opposite bank and capture a miniature bridgehead. Even though the Soviets faced only weak Estonian security and construction units, they were not able to exploit their initial success. Their main problem was perhaps the fact that the segment of the river they were trying to cross had not frozen solid and the ice had been broken into pieces. The only way to transfer men to the other side was by boats but the rubber ones were too small and could carry only a handful of men while the rafts and larger fishing boats the troops were able to find were just too few in number. On the top of that, the Estonian defense was quite well organized and literally everywhere the Soviets were met with murderous machine-gun fire. Given the above, it was not a surprise that they could not reinforce or resupply the sole company fighting on the left bank and, by 7 February, it was wiped out.

THE SECOND SOVIET OFFENSIVE

The initial Soviet assault on the Narva front, apparently, was a total failure. Fedyuninsky and his staff had made a grave error that would cost them the battle. Instead of carefully reconnoitering the German positions, they launched a series of poorly coordinated attacks without any realistic assessment of the strength of the enemy awaiting them. General Govorov was especially irritated by the fact that the attacks in question had been carried out with very little, if any, artillery and tank support. The wrong tactics used by Lieutenant-General Fedyuninsky led to nothing but heavy losses among the rifle divisions of the 2nd Shock Army (during the first five days of February they had lost 1,425 killed and 3,611 wounded) and denied him a spectacular victory.

A new battle plan was necessary. The General Govorov and his aides in the HQ of the Leningrad Front decided to rearrange the forces of the 2nd Shock Army and then to continue the pincer attacks with increased strength.

The plan in question was a very ambitious one: it called for a double envelopment of the entire Axis force defending the Narva area. Two pincer arms would encircle the town itself by attacking simultaneously north and southwest of it. In the meantime, a third pincer arm would strike from the Narva bend straight to the north with the objective of reaching the Gulf of Finland. In so doing, the rear communications of the Axis force would be cut off once again and a second barrier would be placed in its retreat path. That third pincer arm consisted of Fedyuninsky's strongest formation, the rested 30th Guards Rifle Corps which would enter the battle after two weeks of reconstitution and replenishment.

* * *

The Soviet offensive resumed on 11 February. It was preceded by a powerful artillery and aerial preparation. This time the aerial strikes were not only very well planned and executed, but were also continuous – they were carried out with undiminishing intensity throughout the entire operation. The close-support units of the 13th Air Army and the Red Banner Baltic Fleet repeatedly strafed the enemy positions while the fighters provided reliable protection. Especially effective, as usual, were the Il-2 Shturmoviks. Their crews had a variety of targets to choose from: firing points, artillery and mortar batteries, tanks and motor vehicles, rear-area objects and communications and even vessels in the Gulf of Finland.

The artillery bombardment was designed to have a devastating effect on the enemy. It was delivered simultaneously by 3,000 guns and mortars. In a matter of just 30 minutes they fired about 50 boxcar loads of ammunition.

Then the Soviet infantry stepped forward. Fedyuninsky's riflemen experienced difficulties right from the outset. As everywhere, the ice on the river was broken up making the transfer of men and material to the other side a nightmarish undertaking. The swampy terrain hampered the movement of tanks and the maneuvering of the artillery. The supply chain was also affected by the road conditions and ammunition was often carried by hand, literally one shell at the time. The close artillery and aerial support was hampered, too, because light snow obscured visibility and the forward air controllers and artillery observers were hindered in picking up targets.

The biggest success on Day 1 was achieved by the 30th Guards Rifle Corps. During the first hours of the offensive the guardsmen of Lieutenant-General Simonyak destroyed the German bridgehead on the eastern bank of the river at Dolgaya Niva. Wasting no time, they moved across and secured a bridgehead of their own. The river bend at the Krivasoo swamp was cleared rather quickly; the Germans and the Estonians in the trenches were eliminated with hand grenades and bayonets. Then the forward two guards divisions continued their advance to the north. Neither the vigorous German counterattacks and fierce artillery bombardments, nor the knee-deep snow could stop them. The German 170. Infanterie-Division, which provided the backbone of the Axis defense in that area, had no other choice but to fall back.

On Day 2 the drive of Simonyak's corps toward the Baltic coast continued unabated with their close-support artillery playing a vital role in their rapid advancement through the marshy, forested land. The direct-laying guns accompanied the forward infantry and reacted very quickly when enemy firing points and troop concentrations were encountered, literally shooting them to pieces. The good progress of the corps also allowed it to consolidate its efforts with their right-hand neighbors, the 109th and 122nd Rifle Corps.

On 13 February Simonyak's spearheads severed the Narva–Tallinn railroad somewhere west of Auvere. The Gulf of Finland was just a stone's throw away. But the German defense stiffened even further and the Soviets gained no more ground. But what actually stopped the seemingly irresistible advance of the Guardsmen? First and foremost, it was the quick reaction of the German commanders who immediately moved tactical reserves to the endangered zone. In this they were helped by a road network that was much better developed near the seacoast than in the mainland. The rapid maneuver by AFVs proved to be especially important because it allowed the Germans to set up a flexible defensive belt of panzers and assault guns. At Auvere there was also a fixed defensive position made of earth bunkers and stone buildings. Secondly, the Soviet spearheads had very little artillery and no tanks at all due to the vast marshy area they had just covered. In other words, they had no effective means of eliminating the panzers and bunkers.

* * *

Stalin, who was trying to force the Finns to the peace table, was not happy with the slow progress in the Narva area and demanded prompt action.

Govorov decided to gamble and ordered a landing operation at Meriküla. By doing so, the Leningrad Front intended to outflank the 'Panther' Line and so complete the encirclement of Armeeabteilung 'Narva'. Upon securing the beachhead, the landing party was to strike southwards and establish contact with the spearheads of the 2nd Shock Army.

The amphibious assault took place in the small hours of 14 February. It was a total disaster. Apparently, the Soviets had counted on the surprise factor and expected to infiltrate quickly into the enemy rear. Instead, right from the outset their marine battalion encountered very stiff opposition from a mixed battle group composed of Kriegsmarine personnel, Estonian policemen, units of the 'Nordland' Division, coastal artillery, Flak auto-cannons and a handful of Tiger tanks. After several hours of very brutal fighting the landing party was completely decimated. The battlefield was littered with the dead bodies (up to 300) of Red marines. Dozens more were found in the cold waters of the Baltic. The Soviets losses were appalling: 418 (out of 432) marines were killed, another eight captured and only six succeeded in reaching friendly lines. At least three of the Soviet vessels were lost due to mines and artillery fire.

The Soviet High Command was furious at the failure of the landing. Admiral Nikolay Kuznetsov, the commander-in-chief of the Soviet Navy, whose brainchild was small-scale amphibious assaults like this one, heavily criticized the leadership of the Red Banner Baltic Fleet. In a directive dated 18 February 1944 he stressed the following issues:

1. The naval detachment carrying the marine battalion didn't provide any artillery support for the landing.
2. The enemy defenses were not reconnoitered. No enemy opposition was expected.
3. Many of the gunboats left the landing zone prematurely. Their actions during the amphibious assault were considered irresolute.
4. The air units of the Red Banner Baltic Fleet didn't launch any aerial strikes against the landing zone.
5. The commanders leading the amphibious assault had no knowledge of the terrain ahead of them.

The Meriküla landing operation was the culmination of the Soviet offensive efforts in the Narva area. A stalemate was reached, even though the 2nd Shock Army continued their attacks for two more weeks.

* * *

The right flank of the 2nd Shock Army also failed to achieve their goal, which was to outflank Narva to the northwest. On the morning of 11 February, the 43rd Rifle Corps attempted to force their way across the river on a wide front. At some places the Germans managed to push the Russians back, but at two points the attackers succeeded in reaching the opposite bank by quickly crossing the Narva over the ice. Thus, two bridgeheads came into being: one at Riigi, and one between Vepsküla and Siivertsi.

None of the attempts by the Soviets to expand and consolidate these bridgeheads during the following days were successful. The Germans were well aware of how dangerous these enemy footholds might become and did everything possible to contain and then to destroy them. Various elements of the III. SS-Panzer-Corps and the 227. Infanterie-Division were put on alert and committed to battle. Individual Tiger tanks and assault guns also arrived. The resolute counterattacks of the German, Dutch and Scandinavian combatants succeeded in containing the dangerous enemy penetrations and then, step by step, began to push them back. The Soviets responded by sending reinforcements across the ice, as well as with powerful artillery barrages from the far side of the river.

Both bridgeheads were hard nuts to crack. The one at Riigi, for instance, was only 500 m long and no more than 80 m deep, but at the same time was heavily fortified. The Soviets had incorporated in their defensive perimeter nearly all fortifications of the 'Panther' Line they could occupy, in particular the steel and concrete bunkers, and especially the deep trenches. Furthermore, the Soviet company holding the perimeter had an extra number of machine guns which allowed it to establish a defensive system based on strongpoints. It was also supported by a considerable number of artillery batteries positioned on the eastern bank of the river.

The elimination of the Riigi bridgehead was entrusted to a battalion of the newly formed Estonian 20. SS-Grenadier-Division. Determined not to allow the much-hated Soviets to invade their country again, the Estonians threw themselves into the battle with all their might. On 24 February all hell broke loose. The Estonians formed assault groups and launched eleven consecutive attacks. All of them were

A Tiger of schwere Panzer-Abteilung 502 knocked-out in February 1944 at Siivertsi, just to the north of Narva. (TsAMO)

beaten back with heavy losses by their opponents. The twelfth attack, which took place late in the evening, however, was finally successful. Some Estonian assault groups at last succeeded in penetrating into the Soviet trenches where immediately a brutal grenade battle broke out. Thus, the fate of the bridgehead was sealed and before long it collapsed. The Soviet company defending it was completely decimated, losing about 90% of its strength (65 killed). The Estonians, in turn, claimed to have counted about 250 dead bodies on the battlefield, as well taking 30 prisoners. It was quite possible that their report was correct, too, because their opponents had sustained bloody losses during the preceding days and weeks.

In contrast, the Soviet units defending the Vepsküla–Siivertsi bridgehead withstood the severe Axis pressure and held out for two more weeks.

THE SOVIET MARCH 1944 OFFENSIVE

It didn't take the Soviets long to realize that the Narva position was a hard nut to crack. Consequently, the offensive was halted to give the 2nd Shock Army a break to allow its totally exhausted troops time to recuperate. But switching over to the defensive for good reasons was not an option for Stalin. On the contrary, he sanctioned the redeployment of two more armies (8th and 59th) from the southern flank of the Leningrad Front to the Narva sector. Apart from that, strong formations were released from the Stavka reserves, namely the 3rd Guards Tank Corps and the 8th Estonian Rifle Corps. The assignment of the former – a total of about 200 tanks and self-propelled guns – was to break into open country once the German defenses had been breached and quickly advance toward Tallinn. The latter was deployed at Narva for reasons that had much more to do with grand politics than with the actual military situation. It consisted mainly of ethnic Estonians (about 80% of the enlisted personnel) and was needed more for propaganda purposes, i.e. to show that the Soviet cause was strong in Estonia.

Neither of these formations saw active combat during the battle of Narva. By the end of March 1944 the tank corps entrained for Bessarabia, where it joined the 5th Guards Tank Army. In contrast, the Estonian corps remained at Narva and only its artillery units were involved in combat by firing on the enemy across the river from in-depth positions. The 8th Corps was committed as combat force only in September 1944, when it became clear that Germans were already leaving the country. Apparently, as an ethnic military formation, it was seen as untrustworthy by the Soviet High Command and it had been raised as a show unit to promote the use of Estonian troops.

* * *

For the first time, on 1 March, the positions of the Armeeabteilung 'Narwa' were attacked simultaneously by two armies. In the middle the 2nd Shock Army once again attempted to cut off the rear communications of the Narva bridgehead by attacking towards the Baltic shore from the footholds at Vaivara and Auvere. In the southwest, the newly-deployed 59th Army struck on a broad front stretching from Sirgala in the north to Putki, at the Narva bend, in the south.

Neither of the armies achieved any significant success. From 1 to 5 March the troops of Korovnikov's 59th Army, for instance, advanced between 2 and 7 km to the west on a frontage of 30 km. As in the other sectors, they were not able to overcome the fierce German opposition. The combination of bad terrain (knee-deep snow, unfrozen swamps, vast boggy terrain with very few roads) and the well-developed web of enemy strongpoints (built mainly on low hills rising 40 to 70 m above the plain) didn't allow them to achieve a decisive breakthrough in a westerly direction. It was very difficult to employ tanks (even in small numbers) and to take a bearing on a map. All this made the actions of the Soviets very easy to predict right from the beginning. Their maneuverability was further limited by repeated Luftwaffe attacks (12 to 40 Stukas) and frequent artillery bombardments (on certain days the 59th Army was pounded by up to 10,000 heavy shells).

As elsewhere, the Germans frequently counterattacked. For example, on 6 March alone the 117th Rifle Corps repelled 15 counterattacks. These counteractions not only broke the momentum of Korovnikov's offensive, but also inflicted heavy losses upon the Soviets. Thus, on the same day one of their regiments was cut off in a forest near Putki. It managed to breakout the following evening, losing about 40% of its personnel.

* * *

Further to the east Fedyuninsky's 2nd Shock Army fared no better. During the first week of the offensive it gained no ground whatsoever and its efforts collapsed in the face of the very determined Axis resistance. To make matters worse, the critically important bridgehead at Siivertsi, immediately to the north of Narva, was lost.

The elimination of Siivertsi–Vepskula bridgehead must be credited not to the Germans, but predominately to the Estonian 20. SS-Grenadier-Division. Its offensive started on the morning of 29 February after an intense artillery preparation, during which more than 2,000 rounds had been fired. The Estonian assault groups attempted to break into the trenches of the two Soviet battalions defending the bridgehead, but were barely successful. Instead, most of them were pinned down by murderous fire coming not only from the enemy in front of them, but also from Soviet batteries deployed on the far bank of the river. On the next day the 20th SS struck again and by afternoon had succeeded in making a minor penetration in the northern flank of the enemy.

The following two days passed without major combat activity. Having realized that his bridgehead was in jeopardy, Fedyuninsky urgently strengthened it with two more battalions. But his response was in vain. On the morning of 4 March the Estonians struck again with a superior force and the foothold began to crumble. The Soviet defense was fragmented and the SS began to eliminate them one at the time. In a desperate attempt to reinforce the hard-pressed foothold, on 6 March Fedyuninsky sent one more battalion across the Narva. This, however, was done in a broad daylight. Almost immediately, the battalion was spotted and the Axis artillery shot the unfortunate Soviet troops to pieces. About 90 dead and wounded Soviet troops remained lying on the ice. Only a portion of combat-fit men reached the western bank.

By nightfall the bridgehead at Siivertsi was completely decimated. The Soviets had sustained terrible casualties. One of their units, for example, had lost 431 killed and wounded, as well as 107 machine guns, 14 artillery pieces and 10 mortars. There is no doubt that the losses of the others were equally heavy.

THE OFFENSIVE AGAINST THE IVANGOROD (NARVA) BRIDGEHEAD

Apart from the desperate attempts of the 2nd Shock Army to encircle Armeeabteilung 'Narwa' by pincer attacks, a direct assault was also mounted on the Ivangorod bridgehead. It was undertaken by the 30th Guards Rifle Corps, which had been pulled out of the Auvere bridgehead by the end of February 1944. Then the badly battered divisions of the corps were given a five-day rest period which they used to replenish and recuperate. They also conducted extensive training exercises emphasizing assault tactics and the coordination of different weapons. Later on, however, these drills were proved to have been insufficient because the troops displayed a shocking lack of basic skills.

During the first week of March 1944 there was only a sporadic activity along the perimeter of the bridgehead, namely occasional scouting raids, probing attacks and artillery barrages. The most fearsome strike was delivered on the evening of 6 March by six Soviet long-range air corps, which represented nearly all of Stalin's strategic air force at the time. Various types of twin-engine aircraft (B-25, Li-2, Il-4, etc.) conducted a total of 674 sorties, dropping hundreds of tons of bombs on the western parts of Narva. By doing this, the Soviet High Command hoped to annihilate the German defenses in the town, and especially the artillery, but the only thing the Red bombers achieved that night was the almost complete destruction of the settlement. The German garrison itself sustained relatively light losses but the baroque old town, built during the Swedish rule in the late seventeenth century, was practically leveled.

* * *

The main offensive of the 30th Rifle Corps was unleashed on the morning of 8 March. It was preceded by a powerful two-and-half-hour-long artillery softening-up, one of the longest preliminary bombardments of the entire war. Then the Soviet ground forces surged forward. They were echeloned in depth: three divisions were in the first echelon, advancing from the northeast, east and southeast, respectively, while the fourth one formed the second echelon, ready to attack at any moment. The first-echelon divisions had formed assault teams comprising infantry and combat engineers. They were accompanied by 45 mm and 76 mm guns, manhandled by their crews, for direct-fire support. The assault teams in question were spearheaded by tanks and self-propelled guns (three regiments in total) with submachine gunners riding on them.

Despite careful preparation, the Soviet onslaught collapsed shortly after it began. The well-entrenched SS troops separated the infantry from the tanks, knocked out the latter and shot to pieces the tank-riders. The Soviet artillery was not able to answer adequately because, having consumed most of their daily ammunition allowance during the preparation, the indirect-fire units were critically short of ammunition and the guns accompanying the infantry turned out to be not powerful enough to deal with the solid German fortifications.

Reloading ammunition in a Pz.Kpfw. V 'Panther' Ausf. D of SS-Panzer-Abteilung 11 'Hermann von Salza' in Narva, early spring 1944. (Mirko Bayerl)

The Soviet leadership was still convinced that the Axis defense could be broken by one major push and decided to continue the attacks during the following night. This time the assault teams were split into smaller groups, designated assault groups and blocking detachments in accordance with the missions assigned to them. Even though in several points the Red infantrymen succeeded in overcoming the barbed wire entanglements and infiltrating into the first trench line, they generally failed in their efforts to capture the strongholds.

On the morning of 9 March the Soviet corps struck again but the SS troops fought back with great vigor. They pinned the attackers down with murderous fire and repelled them with heavy losses in men and materiel. The general picture remained unchanged during the next six days. The Soviets attacked day and night but failed almost everywhere to gain ground. The only exception was the northeastern sector where the Lilienbach dairy was taken after five days of heavy fighting with some die-hards of the 'Nederland' Brigade. As usual, the main problem confronting the Soviet assault groups were the bunkers. Made of steel, concrete or wood, these bunkers proved to be very hard nuts to crack.

On 16 March it became apparent that the Guards Corps would not be able to meet the objective assigned to it and Fedyuninsky ordered Lieutenant-General Simonyak to switch over to the defensive. The bridgehead remained relatively quiet for the following couple of weeks, during which both sides used every opportunity to improve their jump-off positions. The Soviets operated mainly with small assault groups while the Germans repeatedly counterattacked with infantry and tanks. Firefights were also quite common.

* * *

The predictable tactics employed by the Soviets during the first half of March 1944 creates the impression that they had had no idea how formidable the Ivangorod bridgehead really was. It was only on 19 March that the corps' intelligence section at last established a true picture of the enemy's strength and fighting qualities. By then it became clear that the foothold was defended by the bulk of the 'Nederland' Brigade, the 'Denmark' Regiment of the 'Nordland' Division, up to three independent battalions and a powerful artillery arm (40 artillery and 17 mortar batteries plus 6 Nebelwerfers).

The Red scouts and observers found out that the bridgehead was divided into sectors and consisted of six major strongholds:

1. West of Lilienbach (1 concrete bunker, 30 earth bunkers, 5 field guns, 2 AT guns, 1 Flak gun, 2 tanks and assault guns) – 41 firing points in total
2. South of Lilienbach (1 concrete bunker, 41 earth bunkers, 2 concrete shelters, 2 field guns, 6 AT guns, 9 Flak guns, 7 tanks and assault guns) – 66 firing points in total
3. At the eastern outskirts of Ivangorod, between the motorway and the railway (1 concrete bunker, 44 earth bunkers and steel pillboxes, 2 covered artillery emplacements, 7 field guns, 2 AT guns, 1 Flak gun, 3 tanks and assault guns) – 60 firing points in total
4. North of Natalin (1 concrete bunker, 30 earth bunkers, 12 field guns, 3 AT guns, 4 Flak guns) – 50 firing points in total
5. Dolgaya Niva and the nearby factories (2 concrete bunkers, 57 earth bunkers, 4 field guns, 12 AT guns, 4 Flak guns) – 79 firing points in total
6. On the bridgehead, simultaneously protecting the motorway and the river crossing (17 earth bunkers, 4 field guns, 1 AT gun, 3 Flak guns, 10 tanks and assault guns) – 35 firing points in total

What the Soviet scouts didn't know was that the Ivangorod bridgehead had been turned into a fortress thanks to the superhuman efforts of the combat engineers of the III. SS-Panzer-Corps. Night after night the latter moved across the river to build barbed wire entanglements, palings, gun emplacements, machine-gun nests, as well as digging kilometers of full-depth and communication trenches. It was these field fortifications that allowed the SS troops to withstand several Soviet onslaughts and a countless number of artillery and aerial bombardments.

The German accounts also emphasize the role played by the artillery of the SS Corps in the defense of the bridgehead. The artillery regiments of 'Nordland' and 'Nederland', for instance, fired many intense barrages during the first week of February 1944. In so doing they not only kept the advancing Soviets at bay, but at the same time allowed the friendly infantry to man the fortified perimeter in a very orderly manner. The maneuverable 'Stuka zu Fuss' and 'Raketen-Vielfachwerfer' halftrack rocket-launchers also contributed to the German defensive success during the first weeks of the struggle for the Ivangorod foothold. The firepower of the Axis garrison grew even further by the beginning of March 1944, when the Flak battalion of 'Nordland' arrived in Narva from a training ground in Germany. It consisted of three batteries of deadly 8.8 cm heavy pieces and one battery of high-velocity auto-cannons.

Vehicles stuck in mud. Narva front, 1944. (National Archives of Norway)

* * *

No more attacks followed after the fiasco of Simonyak's divisions on 15/16 March. The second battle for Narva was practically over and its results were quite disadvantageous to the Soviets. They not only failed to capture significant ground but also suffered heavy casualties. For instance, from 7 to 28 March 1944, the main formation involved in the assault (30th Guards Rifle Corps) lost 6,152 killed and wounded while another 11 of its troops went missing. There is no doubt that the losses sustained by the combat units supporting the corps' offensive were no less bloody.

Following the failure of the offensive in March 1944, the officers of the corps' operations section carefully dissected every aspect of the battle. The following conclusions were reached:

1. The rest period given to the troops after the withdrawal from the Krivasoo–Auvere area was quite short (just 5 days) and therefore inadequate. They entered the battle undertrained and unprepared for the task assigned to them. The battalions and regiments were not able to carry out independent actions.
2. Attacks were uncoordinated and unsynchronized, in some sectors the infantry remained in their positions, simply refusing to go forward; the infantrymen were not trained to fire while running or moving.
3. The assault groups were very small in size (15–20 men) and therefore not strong enough to make decisive penetrations in the enemy's defense. Their actions could be considered ineffective.
4. The commanders of the infantry units had no idea how to achieve firepower superiority over the enemy while positioning their weapons. They also didn't know how to react in critical situations on the battlefield when quick redeployment of resources was very much necessary.
5. The two-hour-long preliminary bombardment failed to eliminate the enemy firing points and especially the steel bunkers whose thick armor (120 mm) provided excellent protection and stability.
6. The commanders had a poor knowledge of the enemy main line of resistance. In some sectors the no man's land was up to 1,600 m deep, which led to heavy losses among the attacking Soviet forces while trying to cover such a wide open space.
7. Staffs at every level of command didn't know how to collect, analyze and evaluate intelligence data on the enemy and its fire system, nor how to direct their troops on the battlefield.
8. The commanders didn't know how to conduct artillery fire on targets and synchronize it with the actions of their infantry. They tried to accomplish the missions either by attacking only with infantry, or only by means of the artillery, thereby ignoring the basic principles of the combined-arms warfare.
9. The commanders of the units didn't know how to conduct close-quarter operations.

Speaking of casualties, it must be noted that during the first battle of Narva (1 February–25 March 1944) the entire 2nd Shock Army suffered heavily, losing no less than 60,502 men:

- 1–29 February: 10,468 killed and 33,450 wounded
- 1–25 March: 4,135 killed and 12,449 wounded

The materiel losses sustained by the army were also quite heavy: 819 machine guns, 95 artillery pieces, 313 mortars and 58 trucks.

The casualties of the other two Soviet armies involved in the battle of Narva (8th and 59th) during March 1944 were most probably of similar scale. By way of comparison, from 1 to 31 March 1944 the divisions of Armeeabteilung 'Narwa' had lost 16,376 in killed, wounded and missing.

OPERATION 'STRACHWITZ'

As it was previously mentioned, by 24 February the left flank of the 2nd Shock Army had crossed the Narva–Tallinn railroad at the Vaivara train station, some 30 km west of the town. In the meantime, another spearhead of Fedyuninsky's army had reached the same railroad further to the east, at the Auvere station. The Germans, however, remained in control of a narrow salient between them known as the 'boot'. In so doing they had effectively split the Soviet bulge into two parts. Thus, two relatively small footholds came into being, which Fedyuninsky intended to use as jump-off points for the complete encirclement of the enemy forces at Narva. The Germans were well aware what was in store for them, and so did everything possible to contain those penetrations. They even designated them in a very quirky manner, calling them 'West Sack' and 'East Sack', respectively.

The offensive of the 2nd Shock Army from the 'sacks' resumed on the morning of 25 February after a powerful 60-minute artillery preparation. Its objective was

One of the vehicles of the of the reconnaissance battalion of the 'Nordland' Division. Narva front, 1944. (National Archives of Norway)

Spring thaw sets in: this VW staff car of the 'Nordland' Division is stuck in the mud. Narva front, 1944. (National Archives of Norway)

the same – to reach the southern coast of the Gulf of Finland, thereby severing the rear communications of the Narva garrison and completely encircling the latter. But it was not meant to be. The Germans, Scandinavians and Estonians fought back with great vigor and during the day the Red assault groups advanced no more than 200–400 meters. The latter had no remedy against the murderous machine-gun, small-arms and artillery fire they encountered along the entire perimeter, or against the frequent counterattacks supported by Tiger tanks and assault guns.

All further attempts of the Soviets to unite and expand both footholds were utterly unsuccessful. They were stopped dead in their tracks by fierce counterattacks and fanatical resistance put up by various battle groups of the German 61., 170., 227., 'Feldherrnhalle' and 'Nordland' Divisions. The grenadiers, engineers and artillerymen received valuable support from a handful of 'Tigers' of schwere Panzer-Abteilung 502 despite the very tank-unfriendly terrain.

In the first week of March 1944, it was becoming increasingly clear that the entire Narva Operation was heading for a stalemate. In an attempt to turn the tables in favor of his Leningrad Front, General Govorov handed the sector of both 'sacks' to the recently arrived 59th Army. The mission of the latter, however, remained unchanged: to severe the main supply route of the Narva garrison and reach the Baltic coast.

The offensive of the 59th Army went ahead on the morning of 9 March. The change of the leadership, however, didn't lead to a change in fortune for the attackers. By 20 March, when their attacks were canceled for good, they had advanced no more than 400 m in the vicinity of both 'sacks'. Their failure could be explained by many factors. First and foremost, the terrain was nightmarish. The snow was still deep but, at the same time, the swamps had not frozen completely. The area had a poorly developed road network which made it difficult for the supply columns to reach the frontline and for the commanders to maneuver their forces. On top of that, the Germans counterattacked at every opportunity. Their counterattacks were usually supported by massed artillery fire and well-coordinated close air support.

* * *

The final phase of the first battle of Narva was marked by a powerful German counteroffensive aimed at the biggest threat to Axis positions in Estonia: the West and East Sacks.

The buildup for that counteroffensive had already begun in the first week of March 1944, when the crack East Prussian 11. Infanterie-Division was transferred from the neighboring 18. Army. Together with the 227. Infanterie-Division, it was placed under the XXXXIII. Army Corps to complete the preparation for the attack. Since no armored unit could be made available, Armeeabteilung 'Narva' created one of its own. It was designated Panzerverband 'Strachwitz' and comprised nearly all operational AFVs available to the Armeeabteilung. The makeshift armored unit was named after its commander, Oberst Hyacinth Graf Strachwitz, a highly decorated officer who had the reputation of being a daring tactician and one of the best panzer leaders.

First, the leadership of Armeeabteilung 'Narva' decided to eliminate the 'West Sack'. For that purpose it employed not only the above mentioned 11. and 227. Infanterie-Divisions, but also elements of Panzergrenadier-Division 'Feldherrnhalle' and the 61. and 170. Infanterie-Divisions. They were supported by about forty five tanks and self-propelled guns.

The offensive of the XXXXIII. Army Corps started on 26 March with massive artillery and Stuka support. It didn't take the Germans long to realize that, in the week preceding the attack, the Russians had considerably strengthened their defenses.

A soldier of the 'Nordland' Division during one of the pauses in the battle. Narva front, 1944. (National Archives of Norway)

Thus, right from the outset, they were forced to deal not only with the difficult terrain but also with the very fierce enemy opposition. There were many machine-gun positions and log-and-earth pillboxes. There were also formidable anti-tank nests that inflicted some losses on the attacking armor. Nevertheless, the Germans kept chewing their way forward. What worked for them was their superior tactics: the tanks were accompanied not only by infantry, but also by mixed combat teams comprising grenadiers, combat engineers, anti-tank guns, mortars and flamethrower operators. They also maintained constant contact with the artillery and air force, calling them in every time an enemy position had to be blasted.

The ultimate objective of Operation 'Strachwitz' was the destruction of the Soviet river crossings at Krivasoo and the recapture of the western bank of the Narva as a main line of resistance. The determined enemy opposition, combined with the completely swampy terrain (with water levels up to 50 cm), prevented them from achieving their plan. Instead, they managed to encircle the main body of the 109th Rifle Corps (the entire 72nd Division and a regiment of the 109th Rifle Division) in the area south of Vivara. Shortly afterwards General Friessner, the commander of Armeeabteilung 'Narva', reported the complete annihilation of the pocket. But this was not the case. During the night of 28/29 March the encircled group launched a breakout attempt to the southeast. At the same time, a relief force of the 59th Army mounted an attack towards the latter and before long a narrow corridor was established through which the bulk of the trapped units escaped. Their losses were heavy, but not catastrophic: from 26 to 29 March, the 72nd Rifle Division lost 789 men in killed, wounded and missing. It also had left behind most of its heavy weapons: four 76 mm guns, eleven 45 mm AT guns, eighteen 82 mm mortars and seven 120 mm mortars. The losses of the other trapped unit, the 381st Regiment of 109th Rifle Division, amounted to 249 men.

The HQ of Armeeabteilung 'Narva' reported much higher figures, but they most probably include also the damage inflicted on the Soviet forces outside the 'pocket'. In particular, the XXXXIII. Army Corps claimed 1,739 counted dead bodies, 4,400 probable killed, 651 captured prisoners, 37 captured deserters and a considerable amount of booty (24 artillery pieces, 50 AT guns, 32 mortars, 42 motor vehicles, 27 cross-country vehicles, 3 tractors, plenty of ammunition of various types and a lot of small arms) for the period from 26 to 30 March. The flag of one of the regiments of the 72nd Rifle Division also fell into German hands.

Two more figures are worth noting. First, the Germans also claimed the elimination of 350 bunkers and combat positions, which indicates how heavily fortified the

Spring thaw sets in: a VW staff car of the 'Nordland' Division being recovered by horses. Narva front, 1944. (National Archives of Norway)

Soviet positions really were. Second, the losses sustained by them during the four days of mopping up of the 'West Sack' were appalling (2,183 in killed, wounded and missing), which means that the battle was a real bloodbath.

Even though the first 'Strachwitz' Operation didn't fully meet its ultimate objective, it could be considered a tactical success because it reduced the 'West Sack' to the bare minimum. Thus the Russians were deprived of a chance to assemble sizable forces on the western bank of the Narva and from there undertake another pincer attack.

* * *

In the first days of April 1944 the XXXXIII. Army Corps redeployed its troops further to the east with the intention of eliminating the 'East Sack'. Some minor changes occurred in the order of the attacking formation – in particular, the 11. Infanterie-Division was replaced by the 122. Infanterie-Division. It was to be supported by 61 tanks and self-propelled guns (11 Tigers, 20 Pz IV, 25 StuG III and 5 Marder).

The second 'Strachwitz' Operation (codenamed Osterurlaub – 'Easter Holidays') began early on the morning of 6 April. The Soviet defensive perimeter came under murderous bombardment delivered by a vast variety of heavy weapons, including Flak guns, 28 cm mortars and Nebelwerfers. Then the tightly packed German assault teams rolled forward. In the days preceding the onslaught an extensive terrain reconnaissance had been carried out and the scouts had reported that the land was impassible. An attempt had been made to postpone the attacks but it was rejected by Hitler. But once the operation went ahead, it turned out that luck was on the side of the Germans. Their heavy armor used the hard surface of the railway embankment to strike into both Soviet flanks. Before long elements of at least two Soviet divisions were encircled.

A bloody close-quarter battle ensued in the forested swampy area at Auvere. The Germans mercilessly pounded their enemies with heavy artillery, Stuka dive bombers (in daylight) and Hs 123 biplanes (at night time). Their assault teams mopped up the Soviet pockets of resistance one at the time. The 59th Army, in turn, launched relief attacks to rescue the trapped forces. They were more or less successful because the bulk of the encircled Red units managed to come out of the trap. Their losses, however, were considerable. For example, the 80th Rifle Division, which had had two of its regiments surrounded at Auvere, lost 158 killed and 347 wounded in a matter of just two days. Another 368 of its men failed to escape from the pocket.

Given the intensity of the battle, it is perhaps no surprise that the Germans claimed to have inflicted very heavy losses on the opponent: 727 prisoners, 2,141 counted dead and more than 3,000 others probably killed for the period from 6 to 9 April. The amount of booty captured by them was also considerable: 32 tanks, self-propelled guns and SU-76s; 5 artillery pieces, 89 AT guns, 82 mortars (including 57 heavy ones), 50 trucks and tractors. Even more shocking is the enormously high number of enemy bunkers and combat positions destroyed by them – 2,313 – which clearly shows what they had been through during 'Easter Holidays'. Still another indicator was the heavy price paid by the XXXXIII. Army Corps for that limited success – from 6 to 9 April it lost 2,750 men (including 418 killed).

Like the first 'Strachwitz' Operation, the second one didn't fully meet its objective either because the 'East Sack' was not completely eliminated. Nevertheless, its most dangerous part, the top, had been smashed. Now the Narva–Tallinn railway was back in German hands along its entire length. The badly battered grenadiers of the 61. Infanterie-Division were especially happy with the new situation. With both 'sacks' gone, the damned 'boot' that had crippled their strength and had wrecked their nerves no longer existed.

Spring thaw sets in: soldiers of the 'Nordland' Division retrieve a car stuck in the mud. Narva front, 1944. (National Archives of Norway)

Literally all combat branches of Armeeabteilung 'Narwa' distinguished themselves during the second 'Strachwitz' Operation. The heavy artillery, for instance, knew no mercy and pounded the Soviets with up to 23,000 rounds per day. The grenadiers and engineers of the 'Feldherrnhalle' Division fought very bravely while incorporated in various assault teams. The handful of Tigers of 2./schwere Panzer-Abteilung 502 (one of them was led by the famous Otto Carius) were also instrumental in the success of the breakthrough. Needless to say, Hitler was very pleased by the success and commanders at various levels received high military decorations. Carius, for instance, was awarded Knight's Cross, while Friessner received Oak Leaves. But it was von Strachwitz who benefited most – he was both promoted to Generalmajor and decorated with Diamonds to the Oak Leaf of the Knight's Cross, thus becoming the eleventh recipient of the award.

The Finnish general Hugo Osterman (in the center) watches a German Vierling 2 cm anti-aircraft gun on the Pskov front, May 1944. (NAC)

* * *

After the reduction of the 'East Sack' a pause in the battle followed as both sides were in a desperate need of recuperation. The Soviets, who were now under new leadership (on 10 April 1944 the HQ of Korovnikov's 59th Army handed over its sector to the neighboring 8th Army and was pulled out of the frontline), were still in possession of the so-called Krivasoo bridgehead. The German High Command decided to make one last attempt to restore the western bank of the Narva as a main line of resistance and on 19 April the third 'Strachwitz' Operation was unleashed. As usual, it was supported by a considerable number of combat aircraft (more than 100) and massed artillery fire. Furthermore, this time almost every operational AFV of the Armeeabteilung (up to 76 tanks and self-propelled guns) was assembled in the sector of the XXXXIII. Army Corps to support its offensive. Their mobility, however, was restricted by the very boggy terrain.

The German battle plan called for a concentric attack in the middle of the bridgehead aimed at splitting it in two. Subsequently, the remnants would be annihilated separately. Since it was clear that the enemy already had considerably strengthened the perimeter, assault teams were formed once again. As usual, the grenadiers had to be accompanied by tanks and assault guns. Thus assembled, the assault teams had to be spearheaded by groups of 20-30 combat engineers. The mission of the latter was to clear passages in the minefields and blast obstacles, thereby clearing the way for the infantry and the AFVs.

The third 'Strachwitz' Operation began early in the morning of 19 April. It was preceded by a short (just 12 minutes) but intense artillery preparation. This time the Soviets (now under the command of the 8th Army) fought back with great vigor and gave up no more than 800 m of ground. Even the very intense close air and artillery support (up 100,000 rounds were fired by Friessner's heavy pieces) didn't help the attackers to prevail. On 23 April the offensive was called off. The defeat left a very bitter taste in the mouths of the Germans not only because they achieved literally nothing even in strictly tactical terms, but also because their losses were heavier than during their previous two attempts to destroy the 'sacks' – 3,441 men, including 497 killed and 101 missing. With this the First Battle of Narva came to an end. A relatively quiet period then ensued that lasted exactly three months.

CHAPTER 5

THE FALL OF NARVA AND THE GERMAN EVACUATION OF ESTONIA, JULY – SEPTEMBER 1944

THE PRELIMINARY SITUATION

In June 1944 the Red Army launched two large-scale offensives that crippled the German war effort in the East. The first was unleashed on 10 June in Karelia, where Stalin was determined to liquidate the 'the Finnish question' once and for all. The Finns were not able to withstand the overwhelming Soviet pressure and hurriedly retreated to their prewar border with the USSR. The leadership of Finland began seriously considering an armistice.

An even a more powerful blow was delivered on 22 June in Byelorussia, where Army Group 'Center' was annihilated in a matter of less than two weeks. A giant hole emerged in the very middle of the Eastern Front and all of a sudden the southern flank of the Army Group 'North' became its southern front.

This situation directly affected Armeeabteilung 'Narwa'. Since the contact with the retreating remnants of Army Group 'Center' had to be restored as quickly as possible, combat-worthy forces were hurriedly transferred from quiet sectors like the Narva front. Thus, the 170. Infanterie-Division was shipped off with great speed from 28 June onwards. It was followed shortly afterwards by the 225. Infanterie-Division. But this was not all – before long the Armeeabteilung was ordered to give up four more divisions (58., 61., 126. and 227.), getting nothing in return. Even smaller units like the armored reconnaissance battalion of the 'Nordland' Division and schwere Panzer-Abteilung 502 were detached, loaded on trains and urgently sent to the endangered sector. Given the fact that Panzergrenadier-Division 'Feldherrnhalle' had been redeployed to Central Byelorussia already, before the outbreak of the Soviet summer offensive, it can be safely said that by mid-July the Narva sector had been stripped of most of its infantry and nearly deprived of its entire striking power. Even Friessner, the commander of the Armeeabteilung, was not spared. Hitler was dissatisfied by the way Lindemann was doing his job as a commander-in-chief of Army Group 'North' and replaced him with Friessner, who had just been promoted to Generaloberst. General der Infanterie Anton Grasser, the commander of the XXVI. Army-Corps, was appointed Friessner's successor.

Right from the first day Grasser found himself in a precarious situation. On the one hand, it was clear that, despite the reduction of its combat strength, the chief mission of the Armeeabteilung – to keep the Narva River largely under German control – would remain unchanged. On the other hand, Grasser and his staff were aware that every withdrawal would mean yet another shock to the hard-pressed Finnish front. Therefore, only limited shortening of the frontline was possible.

All hopes were now placed on the 'Tannenberg' Line, a fall-back position situated some 30 km to the west of the 'Panther' Line, the construction of which had begun as early as March 1944. It was established along the so-called 'Blue Hills' and from a tactical point of view was constructed in a very smart way. In particular, it allowed the Russians very few opportunities to concentrate and assemble their forces close to the front. Furthermore, it eliminated almost any menace to the flank from the south, keeping the potential attackers out of their most likely penetration zone.

The 'Tannenberg' Line (alternatively known as the 'Narwa II' position) was also very-well fortified. It consisted of full-depth trenches with integrated open machine-gun emplacements and earth bunkers. At several places there were also steel pillboxes. The approaches to the trenches were protected by barbed wire entanglements and minefields. Behind the main line of resistance there were several blindages and command posts.

* * *

Grasser believed that the withdrawal of the main line of resistance to the 'Tannenberg' Line would reduce the front by more than twenty kilometers and would allow him at last to form the much-needed tactical reserve since a whole infanterie-division could be taken out of the frontline. He received approval from Friessner but the withdrawal was refused by Hitler for political reasons (the situation in Finland).

The chief worry of the command of Armeeabteilung 'Narwa' was beyond doubt the absence of any significant tactical reserves. So far it had always been possible to create reserves by stretching the sectors of individual infanterie-divisions. But since the number of the divisions left at the disposal of the Armeeabteilung had been reduced to the bare minimum, Grasser now had no other choice but to rely on improvisations. The three existing Estonian border-guard regiments were combined under Divisionsstab z.b.V. 300 (Special Administrative Division Staff 300). Thus, a makeshift infanterie-division came into being. It was employed in the central sector which was considered the less endangered segment of the Narva front. In the meantime, the creation of three more Estonian regiments was underway but this was

Repair of damaged T-70s of 16th Tank Brigade. (TsAMO)

Repair of damaged T-70s of 16th Tank Brigade. (TsAMO)

hampered by lack of clothing and equipment. They were activated in a piecemeal fashion, literally one platoon at the time. These units, platoon by platoon, were then employed on the front along Lake Peipus, thereby relieving the German units deployed there. Grasser and his staff had no illusions about the overall quality of the Estonian units – lack of training, and in part the complete absence of training, as well as the lack of any combat experience had to be accepted. Not surprisingly, the morale of these troops was quite low: during the summer of 1944, for instance, 6 officers and 923 men deserted from the Border-Guard Regiments 4 and 6 alone.

THE SOVIET PREPARATIONS

The Soviet preparations for the next round of fighting in the Narva area began in early June 1944. In that month alone, the 2nd Shock Army carried out nineteen regiment, battalion and company-level drills and exercises. Special attention was paid to river-crossing attacks and handling boats and other necessary engineering equipment. Fedyuninsky and his staff were satisfied with the results and firmly believed that the troops were well prepared for the upcoming operation.

The HQ of the Leningrad Front issued the basic directive for the Narva Operation on 15 July 1944. The main battle plan didn't differ much from the previous ones: the German group at Narva was to be encircled and destroyed by pincer attacks. The immediate objective of this new offensive was to secure the Auvere area. Subsequently, Soviet spearheads were to advance rapidly to the Purtse River, some 75 km to the west of Narva, where bridgeheads then had to be secured on the opposite bank. In so doing, a firm base for a further advance on Tallin would be established.

The main blow, as usual, was to be delivered by the 2nd Shock Army of Lieutenant-General Ivan Fedyuninsky. Initially, it was made of 5 rifle divisions (divided between two rifle corps), plus several artillery, tank and engineer units. By the beginning of the battle the army numbered 46, 385 men, 1,409 guns and mortars (including the anti-tank and anti-aircraft pieces), and 62 tanks and self-propelled guns.

It is worth mentioning that immediately after the outbreak of the offensive the shock army was massively reinforced with infantry (five rifle divisions were transferred

Pak 40 AT guns of unknown unit of the German 18. Army captured by 16th Tank Brigade on 20 July 1944 near the village of Eliny during the offensive of 3rd Baltic Front against the 'Panther' Line. (TsAMO)

StuG IV assault gun of unknown unit of the German 18. Army; destroyed on 5 August 1944 by the crew of Senior-Sergeant Berezhnoy (16th Tank Brigade) during the offensive of 3rd Baltic Front in the vicinity of Tartu. (TsAMO)

from the neighboring 8th Army), artillery (three artillery divisions), 'Katyushas' (three rocket-launcher regiments), armor (four regiments) and two backpack flamethrower units. This literally doubled the strength of the 2nd Shock Army.

To the south of Fedyuninsky was the 8th Army of Lieutenant-General Philip Starikov. It was to play only a secondary role in this operation and because of that its order of battle had been reduced to the bare minimum: two rifle corps with just five divisions between them, two fortified regions, several artillery units and two armored regiments. The total strength of the army after the transfer of those five divisions to its right-hand neighbor was perhaps about 40,000 men.

THE FALL OF NARVA

The Soviet offensive began early in the morning of 24 July 1944, when the assault formations of the 8th Army attacked at both sides of Auvere, aiming to cut off the rear communications of the Narva bridgehead. It was preceded by a tremendous two-and-a-half-hour-long artillery barrage. The bombardment literally devastated the positions of the III. SS-Panzer-Corps.

The main weight of the attack fell on the positions of the East Prussian 11. Infanterie-Division and the Estonian 20. SS-Grenadier-Division. The bloody battle at Auvere lasted more than twelve hours. Despite their overwhelming superiority, the units of the 8th Army failed to gain significant ground. The East Prussians and the Estonians fought back with great vigor and the Soviets were stopped dead in their tracks. The latter were not only hit hard by the murderous Axis fire, but also were repeatedly counterattacked by the German grenadiers and the Estonian SS. Even the frequent interventions of the Soviet air force, which conducted nearly 300 sorties against artillery positions and troop concentrations, were not able to turn the table in favor of the Red Army. The evening reports submitted to the HQ of the Leningrad Front painted a grim picture: it turned out that during the day the 8th Army had lost no less than 613 killed and 2,254 wounded. Now, all hopes were placed on the 2nd Shock Army.

Fedyuninsky's army joined the battle early in the morning of 25 July 1944 following a devastating 80-minute-long artillery barrage delivered by more than one thousand guns. But, for the defenders, the worst was yet to come – immediately after the end of the artillery preparation masses of combat aircraft of the 13th Air Army and Baltic Fleet littered the sky above the Axis positions. Not surprisingly, by nightfall the latter had been penetrated along their entire length from Narva to the seacoast. The units holding them, the SS 'Nederland' Brigade and the 46th Regiment of the Estonian 20. SS-Grenadier-Division had no choice but to retreat to the west.

Further to the southwest, the 8th Army failed for a second consecutive day to penetrate the very determined Axis resistance at both sides of Auvere. Worse still, once again the Soviet divisions sustained very heavy losses – 814 killed, 2,750 wounded and 30 missing. Marshal Govorov had no choice but to stop all further attacks by the 8th Army. Only the corps on the army's right flank was ordered to strike to the northeast thereby cutting off the main retreat route of the Narva garrison.

* * *

Obergruppenführer Felix Steiner correctly expected the Leningrad Front to resume its offensive after a brief regrouping. Taking into consideration that his troops were not strong enough to withstand the next onslaught, the commander of the III. SS-Panzer-Corps ordered the Narva bridgehead to be evacuated and the fall-back defensive line ('Tannenberg') to be occupied further to the west. Following the instructions of their commander, during the afternoon and evening of 25 July, both Waffen-SS formations ('Nordland' and 'Nederland') successfully abandoned the foothold and began to occupy the 'Tannenberg' Line. The unit covering the withdrawal – SS-Panzergrenadier-Regiment 48 of the 'Nederland' Brigade – however, was not that lucky. It failed to leave its positions in time and was decimated north of Auvere by superior Soviet forces the following day.

StuG III assault gun of unknown unit of the German 18. Army; destroyed on 10 August 1944 by the crew of Lieutenant Razumovsky (16th Tank Brigade) during the offensive of 3rd Baltic Front in the vicinity of Tartu. (TsAMO)

StuH 42 assault howitzer of unknown unit of the German 18. Army captured on 10 August 1944 by the company of Senior-Lieutenant Michailenko (16th Tank Brigade) near the village of Laura during the offensive of 3rd Baltic Front in the vicinity of Tartu. (TsAMO)

The Dutchmen fell victim to the timely decision of Marshal Govorov to turn the right flank of the 8th Army to the northeast. In so doing the left pincer arm (8th Army) made contact with the right one (2nd Shock Army) in the plain west of Narva. The town itself was cleared by the morning of 26 July following bitter street battles that lasted all night long.

The mopping up of the unfortunate SS-Panzergrenadier-Regiment 48 continued throughout 26 July. About 700 men of the regiment, as well as some elements of 'Nordland' and the Estonian division, had been caught in the trap. Some 250 of

A Mk II Matilda of 16th Tank Brigade pictured during the offensive of 3rd Baltic Front in the vicinity of Pskov, July 1944. (TsAMO)

them were taken prisoner by the end of 27 July; the rest were either killed or were still trying to sneak through the Russian cordons. The sacrifice of the regiment, however, was not in vain. The resistance put up by the Dutchmen, Germans and Estonians, although sporadic, disjoined and uncoordinated, prevented the Soviets from closely pursuing Steiner's retreating corps and bought the latter precious time to occupy the 'Tannenberg' Line.

THE ATTACK ON THE 'TANNENBERG' LINE

As result of the annihilation of the rearguard, a large gap emerged in the very middle of the frontline of Armeeabteilung 'Narwa'. The Soviets immediately detected the weak point in the enemy defense and exploited it. Wasting no time, masses of tanks with mounted infantry poured through the gap. The defenders were not able to close it immediately and only managed to check the Soviet advance at the Vaivara train station. Both sides fought stubbornly for every meter of ground, for every bunker and even for every bomb crater. At many places they were engaged in World War

A German AT gun captured at the end of August 1944 by 16th Tank Brigade in the vicinity of Tartu. (TsAMO)

A StuG III assault gun of unknown unit of the German 18. Army; destroyed at the end of August 1944 by 16th Tank Brigade in the vicinity of Tartu. (TsAMO)

I-style trench warfare that differed very little from the bloody battles of Verdun and Passchendaele.

The foreign Waffen-SS volunteers played a crucial role in the containing the Soviet onslaught on 27 July. This, however, was achieved at the cost of heavy casualties. For example, a battalion-sized battle group of the Flemish 6. SS-Freiwilligen-Sturmbrigade 'Langemarck', which had just arrived on the battlefield from Lithuania, lost its effective combat strength after only three days of very heavy fighting. The 'Danmark' regiment of the 'Nordland' division also fought without any rest, but prevented the Soviets from securing permanently the segment of the 'Tannenberg' Line known as the Blue Hills. The Danes simply refused to give up and never took a step back. Furthermore, one of the SS Estonian battalions sacrificed itself to allow the friendly heavy artillery to withdraw to new positions. Speaking of losses, it is worth mentioning that they were quite heavy not only among the ordinary combatants, but also among their commanders. The list of SS officers killed included several junior officers as well as three regimental commanders and the commander of the 'Nordland' division, SS-Gruppenführer Fritz von Scholz.

Men of 16th Tank Brigade, 1944. (Leonid Gorchakov)

The recently promoted Marshal Govorov had no intention whatsoever of allowing the enemy to recuperate. The offensive of the Leningrad Front resumed with growing ferocity by the morning of 28 July. All four divisions of Steiner's III-SS. Panzer-Corps were hit hard. Northwest of Vaivara, 'Nordland', 'Nederland' and the Estonian 20. SS-Grenadier-Division fought stubbornly, as usual. To the south of the Narva–Tallinn railroad the East Prussian 11. Infanterie-Division also stood firm.

The defensive success of Armeeabteilung 'Narwa' further reinforced Hitler's conviction that Estonia had to be held at any cost. His decision making was driven not only by political reasons (Finland), but also by purely economic considerations – Estonia was rich in oil shale reserves and this was of crucial importance for the Third Reich's war machine. Nevertheless, the situation called for desperate measures and at the end of July the production facility was abandoned. The precious equipment was sent to Tallinn while the three heavy Flak batteries protecting the oil shale resources were urgently transferred to the 'Tannenberg' Line. The domestic oil shale industry was abandoned to its fate; before long about 5,000 qualified workers were employed to dig trenches and build field fortifications.

* * *

The failure of the Soviets to breach the 'Tannenberg' Line from the march forced Marshal Govorov to rethink his battle plan. Consequently, on the afternoon of 27 July, he repositioned his forces. The 2nd Shock Army received two rifle corps (five divisions) from the neighboring 8th Army and was ordered to deliver an all-out assault on the 'Tannenberg' Line. The 8th Army, which during the first four days of the battle had sustained ruinous losses, in turn, was tasked with the securing the marshy area to the west and northwest of Putki, thereby outflanking the main German position to the southwest. From that moment on, it played only a secondary role.

Tank crews of 16th Tank Brigade, 1944. (Leonid Gorchakov)

Tank crews of 16th Tank Brigade, 1944. (Leonid Gorchakov)

The town of Tartu

Govorov also decided to give both armies a full rest day to replenish and regroup. It was a risky decision because he was well aware that every pause in the offensive would allow the enemy to recuperate and therefore the entire operation was in danger of becoming a fiasco. On the other hand, the Marshal had already discovered that Steiner's pan-European force was a hard nut to crack and breaching its heavily fortified positions would require proper preparation and large quantities of ammunition.

The offensive of 2nd Shock Army resumed on the morning of 29 July. The attackers formed assault groups that were supported by tanks and artillery. But neither on that day, nor during the following two days, were they able to breach the formidable Axis defense. Steiner's troops conducted active defense: their heavy artillery pounded Soviet assembly areas without mercy while strong tactical reserves, accompanied by tanks and assault guns, repeatedly counterattacked Fedyuninsky's assault teams. This time the Waffen-SS received extensive close-air support: large groups of Stukas and Fw 190s (up to 30 machines) strafed and bombed the Soviet troop concentrations at every opportunity.

It is worth noting that the efficient work of the German artillery and Luftwaffe was facilitated to a considerable degree by the flat terrain below the main line of resistance. It became a true killing field, exposing the Soviet formations to the eyes of the artillery observers and forward air controllers. Evidently the exact location of the 'Tannenberg' Line had been selected very carefully and cleverly.

* * *

In each of those three days the daily losses of the 2nd Shock Army in killed, wounded and missing exceeded the 1,000 mark. It was clear that yet another Fedyuninsky's offensives was bogging down. That's why Marshal Govorov decided to give the 2nd Shock Army some more time to regroup, replenish and recuperate.

Now Fedyuninsky's army was seemingly very strong: by 1 August it totaled twelve rifle divisions (divided between four corps), two artillery divisions, a cannon-artillery brigade, two artillery regiments and five mortar regiments. Its paper strength, however, didn't correspond with the actual condition of the rifle divisions which, as a matter of fact, was desperate. Thus, their infantry was gathered in only 40 battalions which meant that in most of the divisions there were just three battalions (i.e. the regiments had become mere battalions). Not surprisingly, the ration strength of nearly all of the divisions was below 4,000. Even the fact that their attacks would be accompanied by 104 tanks and self-propelled guns, and supported by 1,457 artillery pieces and mortars, could not change the desperate manpower situation.

Steiner also used the brief pause to reinforce his main line of resistance. He employed his strongest formation, the 'Nordland' Division, as a backbone, placing it in the middle of the front. To the south of it, the always reliable 11. Infanterie-Division was deployed. The mission of the latter was to prevent the Russians from outflanking the 'Tannenberg' Line. The remnants of the 'Nederland' Brigade were assembled on the northern flank, near the seacoast, where an enemy offensive was least expected. The Estonian 20. SS-Grenadier-Division was considered less reliable than the other three formations and because of that it was split into battle groups that were assigned to different sectors. Since the combat units of the corps had already sustained bloody losses, the rear-area services were combed out for able-bodied men that were quickly retrained and sent to the frontline to replace the fallen grenadiers. Steiner also didn't miss the chance to set up tactical reserves, as well as to reposition and replenish his artillery.

* * *

The onslaught of the 2nd Shock Army was unleashed on the morning of 3 August following a 90-minute-long artillery preparation. Fedyuninsky was not optimistic about the outcome of the offensive since the only branch in which his army had clear superiority over the enemy was the artillery. Before long events on the battlefield proved his worries correct: the Axis forces fired relentlessly with all their weapons on the attacking Soviet formations; the latter were pounded mercilessly by artillery and Nebelwerfers and badly mauled by constant air attacks. The fiercest struggle was in the central sector where Regiment 'Danmark' fought a battle of life and death against overwhelming odds. The Soviets attempted to secure the so-called Grenadier Hill and Children's Home positions which were considered the cornerstones of the 'Tannenberg' Line, but, as elsewhere, their penetrations were sealed off.

The Soviet offensive resumed with increased aerial support on 4 August. It was another hellish day and for yet another time, Fedyuninsky's assault teams were beaten back with bloody losses. Two quiet days followed during which the leadership of the 2nd Shock Army once again ordered it to regroup and replenish its formations.

On 7 August, the Soviet forces struck again. This time Fedyuninsky attempted to outflank the 'Tannenberg' Line to the southwest by attacking through the marshy area at Putki. But this too was in vain. The East Prussian 11. Infanterie-Division held firm and the Red assault was contained. Marshal Govorov at last realized that German defenses would not collapse and ordered the 2nd Shock and the 8th Army to switch over to the defensive for good.

* * *

Once the attacks were terminated, the operations section of the 2nd Shock Army began to study in detail the reasons for the failure of the summer offensive. The following conclusions were reached:

1. The enemy defenses hadn't been studied well enough by the commanders of the units and formations.
2. Despite the meticulous planning of the artillery support, the counter-battery groups failed to silence the enemy artillery. As result, every time the Soviet infantry stepped forward to attack, it was pinned down by murderous enemy fire.
3. The divisional artillery groups and the counter-mortar group were late in opening fire on the detected enemy indirect-fire artillery elements; i.e. the command and control chain didn't function well and was undertrained.
4. The communication between the infantry and artillery commanders was not good enough.
5. The firing points of the enemy infantry were only partially detected and consequently many of them were not silenced during the artillery preparations.
6. In the course of the fighting, the battalion and regimental commanders displayed poor handling of their artillery units and because of that were not able to eliminate the enemy firing points.
7. The direct-laying guns were not employed in an effective manner. Some commanders didn't know how to position them while fighting in forests, how to maneuver them on the battlefield, or how much ammunition the guns would need while accompanying the infantry.
8. Some divisional commanders didn't know how to use the assigned tanks and on some occasions the latter operated too far ahead of the friendly infantry.
9. The staffs and HQs didn't function well enough. On the top of that, many battalion and regimental commanders had poor knowledge of the battlefield ahead of them.

Heavily damaged Pz.Kpfw. V 'Panther' Ausf. D of SS-Panzer-Abteilung 11 'Hermann von Salza' abandoned in Narva. (TsAMO)

10. Shortly after the outbreak of the preliminary artillery bombardment (5-7 minutes) the enemy carried out its own artillery counter-preparation which the caught the friendly infantry units moving into jump-off positions off-guard and inflicted heavy losses on them. As result, the strength of the assault groups decreased even before the beginning of the main attack.
11. During the opening stage of the battle a considerable number of officers (especially company and platoon commanders) were put out of action by enemy mortar, artillery and sniper fire, which led to breakdowns in the chain of command.
12. The reconnaissance functioned poorly; often the commanders and their staffs had no knowledge of the actual situation on the battlefield.

* * *

Taking Narva was beyond doubt a great tactical and operational success for the Red Army. It ended the months-long stalemate and brought the Soviets closer to the gates of the Estonian capital. It also put additional pressure on the Finnish government and forced it to speed up the armistice talks. At the same time, it was costly in terms of casualties – in July and August the two armies operating on the Narva front lost up to 32,771 in killed, wounded and missing.

The respective war diaries of the Leningrad Front give the following breakdown by army:

JULY 1944

- 2nd Shock Army: 1,776 killed / 5,676 wounded / 106 missing / 7,558 (total)
- 8th Army: 2,395 killed / 9,884 wounded / 159 missing / 12,438 (total)
- Narva front total: 4,171 killed / 15,560 wounded / 265 missing / 12,438 (total)

AUGUST 1944

- 2nd Shock Army: 1,737 killed / 5,919 wounded / 192 missing / 7,848 (total)
- 8th Army: 797 killed / 4,093 wounded / 37 missing / 4,927 (total)
- Narva front total: 2,534 killed / 10,012 wounded / 229 missing / 12,775 (total)

It should be pointed out here that the casualty figures were never published in Soviet/Russian books while those given by 'Western' authors are grossly exaggerated. Thus, for instance, a certain Estonian author, Mart Laar, in his work published in 2006 claims that the Soviet losses sustained during the fighting at Narva and at the 'Tannenberg' Line in July-August 1944 amounted to the unbelievable 35,000 dead and missing, and 135,000 wounded and sick, i.e. way above the total ration strength of all Soviet formations involved in the battle. The same numbers are uncritically included in the work of the British amateur historian Prit Buttar, 'Between Giants', published by Osprey in 2013.

The losses of the defenders were no less heavy. The documents of Armeeabteilung 'Narwa' reveal that from 23 July to 7 August 1944 the German and the Estonian units involved in the battle had lost at least 10,075 men (1,522 killed, 6,585 wounded and 1,968 missing).

Volunteers of the Swedish SS-platoon of the reconnaissance battalion (SS-Panzer-Aufklärungs-Abteilung 11) of the 'Nordland' Division at Narva, summer 1944. (author's collection)

An Estonian Waffen-SS machine-gun crew holds its position during the Battle of the 'Tannenberg' Line, August 1944. Destroyed Soviet tanks are on the right. (author's collection)

The town of Narva after artillery and air raids, spring 1944. (National Archives of Norway)

THE EVACUATION OF ESTONIA

The fate of the 'Tannenberg' Line was sealed not by the events in Estonia, but by the successful Soviet offensives further south. The one launched by the 3rd Baltic Front (the successor of the Volkhov Front) on 17 July proved to be especially decisive.

This Front had been set up in April 1944 and now was led by Colonel-General Maslennikov, the former commander of the 42nd Army. Like most of the Soviet formations operating in the Baltic area, it was very strong on paper but in reality its order of battle was reduced to the bare minimum. Thus, by mid-July, the four armies under Maslennikov (42nd, 54th, 67th and 1st Shock) totaled only 171,100 men supported by 189 tanks, 591 'Katyusha' rocket launchers, 313 anti-aircraft guns, and 4,119 artillery pieces and mortars. Against them General der Artillerie Herbert Loch, the new commander of the German 18. Army, had deployed eight infantry-divisions, each of which numbered up to 10,000 men, plus several smaller units, including some Estonian troops.

Contrary to the German expectations, Maslennikov's armies quickly breached the 'Panther' Line along its entire length. Ostrov fell into Soviet hands on 21 July; Pskov was taken two days later. Shortly afterwards the spearheads of the 3rd Baltic Front entered Latvia and began to turn to the northwest thereby outflanking Lake Pskov (Pihkva). A brief pause followed but on 10 August Maslennikov struck again. On 25 August the 67th Army captured Tartu and in so doing posed a direct threat on the rear communications of Armeeabteilung 'Narwa'. Even though the Germans succeeded in containing the further advance of the Front, the taking of Tartu led to the establishment of a critically important jump off point for further Soviet offensives in several directions. The Stavka didn't miss this opportunity and hurriedly redeployed Fedyuninsky's 2nd Shock Army there.

The final Soviet offensive began on 17 September. The 2nd Shock Army attacked from the Tartu foothold to the northwest; many of its troops were ferried across Lake Peipus directly into the German rear. The 'Tannenberg' Line was now outflanked. It no longer mattered and Hitler had no choice but to sanction the retreat from Estonia.

SOURCES

ARCHIVE MATERIAL

- National Archives, Washington D.C.: Microfilmed records series T311, T312, T314, P-035.
- Tsentral'nyi Arkhiv Ministerstva Oborony [Central Archive of the Ministry of Defense of the Russian Federation], Podolsk: various funds.

PUBLISHED DOCUMENT COLLECTIONS

- Gryler A. N. et al. (Eds.). *Boevoi sostav Sovetskoi Armii.* Vol. 3 and 4. Moscow: Voenizdat, 1990.
- Zolotarev V. et al. (Eds.). *Velikaia Otechestvennaia Voina.* Vol. 16(5-4). Moscow: Terra, 1995 - 2001.

BOOKS

- Dudarenko, M. et al. (Eds.). *Osvobojdenie gorodov.* Moscow: Voenizdat, 1985.
- Escuadra Sanchez, Alfonso. *Feldherrnhalle: Forgotten Elite.* Bradford: Shelf Books, 1996.
- Glantz, David M. and House, Jonathan. *When Titans Clashed.* Lawrence: University Press of Kansas, 1995.
- Haupt, Werner. *Gruppa Armii 'Sever'.* Moscow: Tsentrpoligraf, 2005.
- Krivosheev, E. and Kostin M. *Bitva za Narvu.* Tallinn: Eesti raamat, 1984.
- Newton, Steven H. *Retreat from Leningrad.* Schiffer Publishing: Atglen, 1995.
- Schneider, Wolfgang. *Tigers in Combat,* Vol. 1. Mechanicsburg: Stackpole Books, 2004.
- Tieke, Wilhelm. *Tragedy of the Faithful.* Winnipeg: J.J. Fedorowicz Publishing, 2001.
- Ziemke, Earl F. *Stalingrad to Berlin: The German Defeat in the East.* Washington D.C.: Office of the Chief of Military History, United States Army, 1968.
- *Istoria na Vtorata Svetovna Voina 1939 - 1945.* Vol. 4 - 9. Sofia: Voenno izdatelstvo:, 1978 - 1981.
- *Sovetskie Voenno-vozdusnye sily v Velikoi Otechestvennoi voine 1941 - 1945.* Moscow: Voenizdat, 1968.
- *Velikaya Otechestvennaya Voina 1941 - 1945.* Vol. 3. Moscow: Nauka, 1999.